The Ethical Engineer

THE ETHICAL ENGINEER

Eugene Schlossberger

TEMPLE UNIVERSITY PRESS

PHILADELPHIA

Temple University Press, Philadelphia 19122
Copyright © 1993 by Temple University. All rights reserved
Published 1993
Printed in the United States of America

Library of Congress Cataloging-in-Publication Data
Schlossberger, Eugene, 1951–
    The ethical engineer / Eugene Schlossberger.
       p.   cm.
    Includes bibliographical references and index.
    ISBN 1-56639-056-7 (CL) —ISBN 1-56639-057-5 (PB)
    1. Engineering ethics.   I. Title.
TA157.S383 1993
174'.962—dc20   92-38317

For my brother, Norman

These materials discuss the ethical, not the legal, aspects of engineering and technologically oriented business. These materials must not be used as a substitute for legal advice. Laws change and vary from place to place. Because the engineer and the company both have a duty to obey the law, every recommendation made in these pages should be understood as containing the phrase "provided there is no legal duty to do otherwise."

Contents

PART ONE: *Introduction*   1

  1 The Nature of Engineering Ethics   3
       What This Book Is About   3
       Why Ethics for Engineers?   4
       A Revealing Case   10
           Cut-Throat versus Community Workplaces   11
           The Consumer Life versus the Life of Values   13
           What Should I Do?   18

  2 Ethical Decision Making   23
       The Nature of Ethical Decision Making   23
       How to Use This Book   26
       A Template for Moral Decision Making   29

PART TWO: *Sources of Ethical Decision Making*   39

  3 Values of the Engineering Profession   41
       Safety   45
           Extent of a Risk   46
           Balancing Risks against Benefits   47
           Nature of Risks   49
           Publicizing Risks   50
       Human Progress   58
       Clean, Clear Decision Making   59

Community   60
Partnership with Nature   64
  Environmental Awareness   65
  Environmental Considerations   73

4 Additional Ethical Sources   85
  When to Fight a Battle   86
  Treating Others Fairly and Well   89
  The Duty to Leave the World No Worse   94
  Respect for Persons   105
  Rights   106
  Autonomy   110
  Principles of Accountability   112
  Institutional Duties   114
  Models of the Professions   118
  Promoting Good Consequences   122
  Universality   125
  Moral Precedents   130
  The Golden Rule   132
  Personal Values and the Good Life   134
  When to Break the Rules   135

PART THREE: *Problems and Issues in Engineering*   147

5 Honesty and Professionalism   149
  Whistleblowing   149
  Competence   163
  The Role of Professional Societies   165
  Keeping Accurate Records and Obeying the
    Law   168
  Consulting versus Adversarial Sales   171

6 Good Faith 175
  Conflict of Interest 175
  Confidentiality and Trade Secrets 177
  Patents and Copyrights 181
  Bidding 183

7 Employee-Employer Relations 192
  Types of Work Relationships 192
  Leadership and Healthy Work Environments 194
  Protégés 200
  Dealing with Subordinates 201
  Friendship, Favoritism, and Professional
    Relations 202
  Harassment 207
  Hiring Practices 212
  Interdepartmental Dealings and Hiring away
    from Another Firm 213

8 Special Issues in Consulting Engineering 221
  Advertising 221
    Dishonest or Misleading Advertising 222
    Unseemly or Demeaning Advertising 224
  Competing with Other Firms 225
    Competitive Bidding 225
    Contingency Fees 225
    Bribes and Kickbacks 225
    Derogatory Remarks about Other Engineers 226
  Reviewing the Work of Others 226
    Reviewing the Work of Unlicensed Individuals 226
    Reviewing the Work of Other Engineers 227
  Safety and Liability 228

APPENDIXES   229

Appendix
    1 Two Sample Suggestions   231
            Formation of an Environmental and
                Community Issues Advisory Board   231
            Ethical Ombudsperson   232

Appendix
    2 Summary of Key Points   233

    Notes 251

    List of Cases 279

    Index 281

PART ONE

Introduction

1

The Nature of Engineering Ethics

What This Book Is About

This book is a practical guide to ethical decision making for practicing engineers and others in technologically oriented business and industry. It will help you to make ethical decisions yourself and to understand the reasons behind company policies, legal rules, and professional codes. It is also meant to change the way you think and feel about engineering, so that you can be a better and happier engineer. And it just may cause you to take a new look at the ethical dimensions of life generally.

Unlike many ethics books, this one is geared to finding answers. I have attempted to present clearly and economically some factors you may use in making decisions. To make it easy to use this book as a reference or study guide, I have listed key points in Appendix 2. Of course, there is no such thing as an ethics rule book. Rather, what you need is an ethics construction kit that provides you with tools and materials to construct your own solutions to problems you may face. This book imparts some specific recommendations, many examples of ethical decisions, several tech-

3

niques for ethical decision making, and a variety of rules, principles, and values upon which you can draw. It explains the reasons behind many of the rules and principles and gives you guidance in weighing them.

I have tried to capture and summarize the best in the literature of engineering ethics and also to add a good deal that is new. Some of my recommendations are quite specific, others fairly general. Some of the material will raise new ideas, while some details represent a clear and thorough summary of ''common sense.'' Some of my recommendations are controversial, others are widely agreed upon.

Together, these materials present a comprehensive picture of and guide to engineering ethics.

Why Ethics for Engineers?

Practicing engineers often think that ethical problems are not really their concern. Many ethical decisions are not made by any individual. After all, legal and company rules determine much of what an engineer may or may not do, and committees or executives far removed from the average engineer decide many of the ethical questions that do arise. Of what use, then, is a book or program or course on engineering ethics?

Books such as this one are essential because, for several reasons, engineers must have a clear grasp of engineering ethics. First, many of the ethical decisions that individual engineers must make are not settled by rules. After all, rules do not encompass every situation: often the rules only set limits within which decisions must be made, and some situations are not covered at all.[1] In addition, rules require interpretation. In some cases it may be easy to see which interpretation of a rule is best, but in others it is not so easy. No set of rules or policies can anticipate every ethical problem that may arise, and even the sincerest engineers may need help in understanding the ethical aspects of some situations. So only ethically aware engineers can correctly apply ethical rules to complex situations, keeping to the spirit as well as the letter of ethical rules.

Second, organizations function best when the values implicit in rules and executive decisions are widely understood and discussed within the organization. The best employment situation, both for the employer and for the employees, is a community atmosphere where everyone works together for a common goal in which everyone believes. Companies and firms flourish when their people have common values, a situation impossible to achieve if the rules are bureaucratic mandates handed down from above rather than ways of working toward commonly understood goals. Furthermore, without communication between all levels of an organization, ethical problems may slip between the cracks. Such synergistic effects arise when employees are insensitive to complex ethical dimensions of company operations. It becomes more difficult to overlook ethical problems when each engineer is aware of and sensitive to ethical concerns and potential problems. In general, large decisions are often the resultant of many small decisions made at different levels. Thus, the large decisions reflect the values and ethical aims of the company only when those making the small decisions understand those values and aims and also understand how their decisions fit in with the ethical outlook of the company. In addition, engineers who understand the moral basis of the rules have a greater motivation to obey them, both because they see the rules as morally sound directives rather than as annoying and senseless restrictions and because there is less incentive to make one's own "numbers" look better if the company functions as a community rather than as an arena in which individual "gladiators" can better their own prospects. Moreover, the single most powerful influence on the operation of a firm or company is its corporate climate. John Fleming notes, "An ethical climate involves the total organization and must pervade and infuse all who work for the company."[2] Although the corporate climate is heavily influenced by those at the top, people who advance in the corporation tend to take with them the attitudes they learned before being promoted. And so, Donald Jones advises, "the best time to give ethics training to senior managers is before they become senior executives."[3]

Third, engineers should be sensitive to ethical questions because engineers who understand the ethical dimension of engineering are better and happier engineers. Engineers will be happier in a company in which every engineer understands the value of community, since a community atmosphere requires everyone's participation and it is more pleasant and rewarding to work in a place with a community atmosphere. Engineers who understand the "engineering way" and the values of engineering as a profession, who see engineering as serving a high social goal, will put more into (and take more satisfaction in) their work than those who view engineering merely as a way of drawing a paycheck.

From the employer's standpoint, employing ethically sensitive engineers has several benefits. First, ethics is good business. Ethical sensitivity often avoids costly situations. Although acting ethically often costs more in the short run, acting unethically usually costs more in the long run. Engineers and businesspersons are sometimes tempted to act unethically because the benefits of unethical conduct are immediate and highly visible, while the benefits of ethical conduct are often long-term and hard to calculate. For example, an employer can easily show exactly how much money is being saved when the company denies a worker a $2,000 bonus to which he is entitled. What an employer loses by treating employees unfairly, although real, is more difficult to calculate. The financial effects of a community atmosphere, of employee loyalty, of good engineers coming to work for the firm because the firm has a good reputation, and so forth are indirect. While employee motivation certainly affects productivity, it is impossible to point to the particular extra widgets produced by greater motivation. And no one can calculate precisely how many people refrained from buying Fords because of negative publicity surrounding the Pinto. Acting ethically and responsibly may prevent a costly government regulation, but no line in the budget documents the value of regulations that were not passed. No line in the budget shows the money saved by forestalling litigation as a result of good and fruitful communication with environmental groups. So a standard dollars-and-cents analysis will often fail to take account of the hidden but real costs of unethical decisions. Thus, a good understanding of the ethical dimensions of engineering decisions is a business necessity. Gerald Ottoson contends, "Neglecting to take steps to insure an ethical corporate climate has proven to be an ill-considered risk for many organizations."[4]

Moreover, when firms and companies hire ethically trained engineers they become more marketable. Due to growing concern about ethical issues on the part of the public and regulatory agencies, a company whose engineers are ethically trained has a considerable advantage in public relations. Other companies are increasingly more likely to hire consulting firms that show a strong awareness of ethical issues. Government agencies favor dealing with a company that has a strong ethical profile. Regulatory agencies pay attention to a firm's or a company's efforts to hire ethical engineers or to provide ethical training to the engineers it already employs. Moreover, the public perceives every employee as a representative of the firm or company, and the company or firm is judged by what its engineers say and do, both on and off the job. Ethically aware engineers serve as ambassadors of goodwill, both for their firms and for engineering as a profession.

Companies further benefit from ethically trained engineers who better understand the concerns of environmental groups. A partnership between engineers and environmentalists, based on mutual understanding, is more productive than an adversarial relationship.

Further, companies often desire ethical engineers because ethics makes for better and more productive engineers. Ethically aware engineers are more likely to create a community atmosphere and show trust and fairness in the workplace. In addition, engineering is not just a job but a profession with an ethical dimension. Engineers who see their work as part of a moral project take greater pride and satisfaction in their work, are more productive, show greater loyalty to the firm or company, and are more willing to go the extra mile. When employees regard their work as meaningful, liabilities such as turnover, accidents, and employee theft decrease, while the quality of work output improves.

Finally, since each firm functions best as a community with a shared set of goals and values, it is important that the values implicit in the firm's decisions are widely understood and discussed within the firm. Firms make better decisions when all engineers add their free and informed input.

Hiring and promotion practices illustrate some of these points. The ethical company has a model of what sort of engineer it wants to hire and promote. A company that wishes to make ethical decisions, for example, should give serious thought to the integrity and ethical commitment of an employee. A company that wishes to function as a community will seek to hire and promote team-spirited engineers who consider the needs and welfare of those they supervise. A company that values community will be less eager to promote abrasive, self-centered engineers. If those involved in hiring and promotion decisions do not clearly understand these goals and criteria, the company is unlikely to achieve the personnel profile it seeks. After all, the personnel profile of a company results from many smaller decisions at different levels. Moreover, because traits such as team spirit are difficult to describe or quantize, decision-makers who do not clearly understand the moral outlook of the company cannot apply these criteria correctly. Finally, traits valuable to the company as a whole are not always as clearly and immediately useful to a supervisor. So the motivation for hiring or promoting the right people increases when those doing the hiring understand the reasons for looking for people with these traits.

In sum, the ethical profile of a company depends not only on the rules set by upper-level executives, but also on the ethical outlook and understanding of each and every employee.

A Revealing Case

Here is an example of an ethical problem that no simple rule will solve. It is a problem that any engineer might have to face. And the problem must be solved by the individual engineer, not by a committee or a superior. The case also serves to illustrate why ethics should matter to you and how to think through an ethical problem.

Case 1: While eating lunch in the cafeteria, you overhear Smith, the supervisor of another department, speaking to another engineer. Smith says that Jones appears to be on a fast track and may soon prove a rival for promotion. So Smith intends to lie to Garcia, Jones' supervisor. Smith is going to tell Garcia that he continually hears Jones saying that Garcia is incompetent and that Jones tells everyone that she would do the job much better than Garcia. You realize that this false "confidential" information will not appear in Jones' evaluations or personnel file and that Jones will have no chance to answer this false accusation. What, if anything, should you do about this?

Discussion: Your first response might be, "This is not my problem. Why should I care what happens to Jones?"

In a broader sense, you are asking, "Why should I care about ethics in the workplace?" The answer to this question relates directly to nearly everything discussed in this book. I suggest that if you do not care about Jones and if you do not care about injustice, then you are not only doing wrong: you are also hurting yourself. You must understand how you hurt yourself by not caring about ethics, for the two points made in the following pages lie at the center of engineering ethics. In the short run, ignoring ethics is often profitable. It sometimes seems more practical not to do the right thing. But, as I suggested above, in the long run, if you are not ethical, you will pay for it. From the corporate standpoint, as we saw, ethics is good business. From the individual's standpoint, you are better off doing the right thing. So, before you read about what to do in Case 1, let us pause a minute to consider two major reasons why you are losing out if you do not care deeply about ethics.

Cut-Throat versus Community Workplaces

Two sorts of workplaces exist: the cut-throat workplace and the community workplace. In a cut-throat workplace, people are concerned only about themselves, about advancing their careers or getting by as easily as possible. In a cut-throat workplace, people will lie, stab each other in the back, sabotage projects, and exploit each other. In a community workplace, people care about each other because they are working toward common goals based on common values.

Clearly, working in a cut-throat workplace has major disadvantages. First of all, it is not much fun, nor is it conducive to good work, to deal with people who distrust each other. If you are always wondering who is about to do what behind your back, and if your fellow workers are only out for themselves, you will not enjoy coming to work, and you will do less than your best. If nothing else, you will spend too much time protecting your back. This drawback is especially serious for engineers, since good work requires teamwork, and teamwork requires trust. Moreover, in a cut-throat workplace, where work is merely a means of drawing a paycheck, the forty or so hours a week one spends at work seem like unrewarding drudgery. In a cut-throat workplace, engineering becomes just a series of tasks, rather than a worthwhile project. After all, no one would put changing the oil in her car on her list of favorite ways to spend a Saturday afternoon. Yet, for many people, being part of a winning racing team is exciting, even if one's job on the team is to change the oil. Regarded merely as a task, changing the oil is a chore. Regarded as part of a cherished project, it can be fun and rewarding. The same is true of engineering. The engineer who takes pride in being part of the team developing a socially useful product will enjoy his work. The engineer who views his work as just pushing keys on a computer will not. Since work constitutes such a large part of one's life, the difference between a community workplace and a cut-throat workplace can mean the difference between a happy life and an unhappy one.

Thus, any thoughtful engineer cares very much about the corporate environment. It should be important to you whether the company for which you work is a place in which people sabotage and exploit each other or a place characterized by honesty and fair dealing. It makes a big difference whether you work in a cut-throat or a community workplace. But establishing a good community atmosphere requires everyone's participation. So by caring about other people, and acting to promote fairness and decency in the workplace, you are helping yourself. By contrast, if you do not care about Jones or injustice in the workplace, you are fostering a cut-throat, not a community, workplace.

The Consumer Life versus the Life of Values

Jones is your problem for another important reason. A person may lead one of two kinds of lives: one way becomes a dead end; the other way requires caring about what happens to Jones.

Consider two different ways of leading one's life. We can live "consumer lives," or we can lead lives dedicated to intrinsic value. The consumer life centers on personal enjoyment or "goodies" of one sort or another: a consumer life is just one "kick" after another. The consumer need not be "materialistic": the commodities he seeks may be love or personal excellence. The point is that he regards them as commodities. He does not, for example, regard human love as a good thing for its own sake, as intrinsically valuable whenever it occurs. Rather, he wants to be loved as one might desire to own a television or a trophy, so as to feel prosperous in the goods of life. He wants love as one might desire a sofa, a massage, or a piece of chocolate cake—namely, for the good feeling one gains from consuming or owning them. Of course, everyone enjoys an occasional "goodie." Enjoying your VCR does not mean you are living a "consumer life." The point is that the "consumer" is driven by the restless need to satisfy personal desires for a Mercedes, a VCR, fashionable clothes, power, excellence at tennis, or whatever. He sees fame, love, and personal accomplishment only as goods to be obtained to satisfy his personal desires, and the thrill of obtaining them gives his life its meaning.

Put another way, the consumer has desires but no values. What we *desire* is what we want for ourselves, what it makes us feel good to have. For example, if I desire courage, then I want to be courageous, and it makes me feel good when I am courageous. What we *value* is what we think good for its own sake, quite apart from ourselves. If I value courage, then I want others to be courageous, and I am pleased by courageous acts that have nothing at all to do with me. In short, because I believe in courage, I want the world to be a courageous place. Of course, we usually also desire what we value. If courage is a valuable thing, then of course I want to be courageous. The point is that some people want to be loved because they value love. The consumer does not value love, he merely wants it.

We are constantly being urged to pursue the consumer life. If we listen to advertisements on television, we might think that life is about having sexy nails or about grabbing a six pack of beer and a six pack of women, as one commercial seems to suggest. But the consumer life is a recipe for failure. Anyone who lives the consumer life is necessarily isolated and unhappy.

The consumer is necessarily isolated because no one else can feel what you feel, and so enjoying "goodies" is basically a private project. If you are a consumer, other people serve only as a way of getting commodities. If your goal in life is to enjoy "goodies," what kind of marriage can you have? Since you only care about obtaining goodies, what can your spouse be for you but a tool to help you obtain consumables, to help you feel more personally excellent, or to provide sex, or financial support, or affection, or amusing company? In short, you and your spouse are allies only as long as you remain useful to each other in acquiring your own private goodies. The moment you become a net liability in your spouse's search for goods, your spouse will leave you. After all, you are merely a tool. Why keep a tool that no longer works? Thus, you are basically alone in life, no matter how many friends you seem to have.

The consumer is necessarily unhappy, since the consumer life is by nature a losing game. Once a "goodie" is obtained it loses its allure, and so the consumer is always restlessly moving on to the next "goodie." Success does not last, since goodies do not last and there are always more goodies to be gotten. Perhaps you worked hard through college, hoping to earn enough money in your career after graduation to buy an expensive sports car. Finally you earn $60,000 a year. You buy the sports car, and every morning you walk out on the driveway and say, with a thrill in your voice, "This baby is mine." You feel great—for a week. But before long, you take the sports car for granted: it is just your car. You need a new kick. If only you earned $100,000 a year, you could buy that new house. So you work hard, and finally you buy the house. You wake up in the morning, look around you, and say, "This house is mine." You feel great—for a month. But before long, you need a new kick. If only you earned $150,000, you could buy an Olympic-sized swimming pool.

The cycle is endless because a commodity, once enjoyed, is gone, and you must start over from scratch. The more you have, the more it takes to produce the thrill. Your first car gives you more of a thrill than your tenth. (The life of the consumer, though more respectable, in many ways resembles that of the drug addict.) So you will be forever dissatisfied, no matter what you have, unless you have everything, in which case you will be bored. Either you never have enough, or you have so much that you are desperately looking for something else to want.

The point is that the consumer life lacks structure and so shows no progress. For example, if my goal is to further knowledge for its own sake, then each small step I take has meaning in a larger enterprise, and later in life I could find satisfaction in knowing that I had played some part in expanding the horizons of knowledge. The consumer life does not allow for this: buying two sports cars brings one no closer to a goal, for the only goal of the consumer life is having more goodies, and the number of goodies is endless. The consumer life, thus, is a barren life. Either the consumer is either dissatisfied, always hungry for more no matter how much he has, or he feels jaded and bored when there is nothing left to hunger for. There is simply no way to win at this game.

The alternative is to lead the life of values. Instead of seeking "kicks," one may be driven by a recognition of value, committed to things that are good for their own sake, independent of one's having them. I might, for example, value understanding as a good thing—worthwhile for its own sake—and dedicate my life to understanding. If I do so, I become immediately invested in other people's lives. After all, if I value understanding for its own sake, then what I want is not just for me to understand many things, but also for this world to be full of understanding. Then my goals and projects mean that I care about other people's understanding, about the frontiers of human knowledge. I have a stake in other people's education. I am happy and satisfied to the extent that I learn something, because I view learning Spanish or quantum physics as a step in a larger process. Moreover, I am happy and satisfied to the extent that others learn, since I value understanding itself, quite apart from anything that happens inside my own head. It means something to me if scientists I will never meet learn something about the structure of the atom that I will never understand.

Similarly, if I value excellence at tennis for its own sake, I appreciate excellence in other tennis players and have a stake in their becoming good at the sport. Put another way, I see myself not as an isolated player playing my own game but as part of a communal project, a joint human enterprise pushing toward the unknown, or pushing toward new heights of excellence at tennis. My fellow citizens and I are mutually invested in each other, because we are dedicated to a common goal and because we all see the knowledge and tennis skills each of us gains as good things in their own right.

This is why it is so important for the engineer to see engineering as a calling, to embrace the values of the engineering profession. The engineer who does so is not alone, for she is part of the engineering community. Every engineering advance, no matter who makes it, is a personal victory. Because she values human excellence for its own sake, the engineer takes pleasure in every form of human excellence and sees her own life not as a collection of meaningless events but as progress toward a worthwhile goal, the search for excellence. And every other engineer who values excellence wants her to succeed, because they are all part of the same team, striving for a common goal. Her life is meaningful and happy.

I suggest, then, that the only life not doomed to misery and failure is the life of commitment to value, a life that gives us a stake in each other because we are committed to a common enterprise. If I lead a life committed to value, I care about things like injustice. So I will care about what Smith proposes to do to Jones.

What Should I Do?

To avoid being lonely and frustrated and to avoid working in a cut-throat workplace, you have to care about justice and fairness, and you have to care about the corporate environment. These things affect you and are morally important. To the extent that you commit to these things, Smith's plan is your enemy. So in a very real sense, this *is* your problem.

That you recognize Smith's plan as your problem does not necessarily mean you ought to *do* anything. Part of being an ethical engineer is knowing which battles to fight and which to sit out. In some cases, doing nothing may be the ethically appropriate choice.

The point is that you have to make an ethical choice

here—you must give serious thought to what is right. A careful moral decision is called for. A wide range of choices confronts you, including doing nothing, sending an anonymous note to Jones, having an informal chat with Jones, speaking with or sending an anonymous note to Garcia telling her that Smith's claim is false, threatening to expose Smith if he carries out his plan, speaking to your own supervisor, and lodging a formal complaint against Smith. What should you do?

To simplify matters, we will consider four options: do nothing, speak to Garcia, speak to Smith, and speak to Jones. There are, of course, many ways you could do each of these. Even if you decide, say, to speak to Jones, you must decide how to play it. Ethical thinking requires creativity in part because of the enormous variety of circumstances and possibilities that engineers confront. In fact, in virtually all of the cases we will look at, there are more options and factors than I can discuss. I can merely show you some of the relevant factors and possibilities and how they play out.

If the threat to Jones is minor, and if you are not in a position to do much about it, you may decide to sit this one out, since you are not directly involved (it is not your department, you are not being asked to carry out an immoral order, and you are not responsible for overseeing personnel matters). For example, if Garcia is very fair minded, knows what Smith is like, and so is likely to ignore what Smith says, the best course may be to stay out of it. "Don't fix what ain't broke," as the saying goes. (See "When to Fight a Battle" in Chapter 4 for further guidance.)

Suppose, however, that the threat to Jones is serious and you are in a position to do something about it, so you decide that you cannot, in good conscience, do nothing. Which approach is morally best?

There is no simple rule for deciding this, but you can evaluate ethically the options open to you. You could speak directly to Garcia; however, there are four reasons for not choosing this option. First, Garcia will not know what to make of your claim, since it will be your word against Smith's. Second, fairness to Smith requires that you hear his side of things before reporting him. After all, you may not know the whole story: it is always possible that something Smith has to say could change your whole view of things. (See ''Treating Others Fairly and Well'' in Chapter 4.) Thus, by going directly to Garcia, you are being unfair to Smith. Third, Jones ought to have some voice in what happens, since she is most directly involved; by speaking with Garcia you deprive Jones of the opportunity to take responsibility for her own fate. Thus, going directly to Garcia would violate Jones' autonomy. (See ''Autonomy'' in Chapter 4.) Fourth, by involving Garcia you disrupt the normal operation of that department and its channels. While it is sometimes necessary to do this, it is always preferable, when feasible, to respect proper channels.

These reasons suggest that you should speak to Smith or Jones before Garcia. Should you go first to Smith or to Jones? If you approach Jones first, you are being unfair to Smith, since you give him no chance to present his side. But if you go to Smith first, you violate Jones' autonomy. Since there is a good reason not to speak first to Smith and a good reason not to speak first to Jones, we have to weigh these reasons and see which, in this case, is more important.

On the one hand, because Jones is not Smith's peer or superior, talking to Jones first is unlikely to cause severe harm to Smith: usually, fairness to Smith will not be severely compromised by speaking to Jones before Smith. On the other hand, since talking to Smith might have important consequences for Jones' career, it should be Jones, not you, who decides whether and how Smith is confronted. Usually, Jones' autonomy would be severely undermined if you spoke to Smith before you spoke to Jones. However, if you have reason to believe that, if you spoke privately to Smith about the matter, Smith would not "take it out on" Jones, or if you have reason to believe that Smith could be seriously hurt if you tell Jones what you heard, then you might weigh these factors differently. Moreover, if a few informal words reminding Smith of his ethical obligations would deter him, that would be the best solution for all involved.

So, ordinarily, the best course would be to speak to Jones first, telling Jones that you are willing to discuss the situation with Garcia if Jones wants you to. However, in some circumstances it would be better to talk to Smith privately and, if you are not satisfied, then speak to Jones. Although it is generally better to handle this situation informally, in some circumstances using formal channels is preferable. You must ask yourself to what extent there are significant legal ramifications and to what extent using formal channels would protect you, Smith, and Jones.

In general, your decision must be influenced by factors such as these: How responsive to ethical concerns are the individuals involved? Are there likely to be vindictive repercussions for you, for Jones, for Smith? Are you likely to do more harm than good by taking action? Do you know any of the individuals well? For example, if you know Garcia well and know that she will not jump to conclusions, it might prove best to voice your concern to her, knowing that she will not take any action until she investigates thoroughly, in a way that is fair to both Smith and Jones.

In short, although general considerations can provide guidance, your decision must take into account the character of the corporate setting and the individuals involved. Thus, each case is somewhat different and requires judgment in weighing a variety of factors.[5] No rule book concerning personnel matters can tell you what to do in every case.

2

Ethical Decision Making

So far, we have considered why ethics is important for engineers and discussed how to resolve one particular case. It is time to talk more generally about how to make ethical decisions.

The Nature of Ethical Decision Making

Case 1 from the previous chapter reveals much about the nature of engineering ethics. Ethics is about how to live, about what makes for a good person and for a good life. Ethical thinking is deciding what really matters in life. So every choice you make is an ethical decision. For example, if you choose not to take a promotion in a distant city in order to remain close to your aging parents, you are deciding that some values, such as family ties or helping those you love, are more important than others, such as career satisfaction or the pleasure of the sauna you would be able to purchase if you took the promotion. This decision reflects what matters in life—what is really good and worthwhile—and that is what ethics is about.

Because values cannot be precisely measured like steel rods, ethical decisions always involve a lot of individual judgment. Ethical decisions are not algorithmic.[1] Nevertheless, ethical choices are not arbitrary: deciding what is right is not like choosing between hot fudge and strawberry topping. Making an ethical judgment is more like buying a car. There is no simple answer, usually, to the question of which is the best car for you. But there are good decisions and bad ones, and good decisions result from carefully and reasonably weighing the relevant factors. Safety, cost (both initial and upkeep), cargo capacity, aesthetics, and reliability are all considerations. There is no mathematical formula for weighing safety against reliability, and individuals' needs vary. For example, while it is generally cost-efficient to spend somewhat more for a car that will last a lot longer, it may make more sense to buy the low-cost, short-lived car if you expect your income to rise dramatically in the next few years (since, by the time you are ready to scrap the car, you can better afford a new one). Reliability may be less important if you live on a bus route to work, and cargo capacity is more important for some people than for others. So while you can give advice to a friend that will help her make a wise choice, there is no simple rule book you can give her that will make the right choice for her. There is probably no single ''right'' decision for her. Nonetheless, suppose she has a large family and a job for which being a few hours late might cost thousands of dollars. If she buys (as the family's only car) an unsafe, expensive, unreliable two-seater car because it ''looks good,'' she is clearly making a bad decision.

Ethical decision making is also much like legal reasoning. A judge who must decide a difficult question of law draws on a variety of sources, such as statutes, precedents, and legal maxims, using the tools of legal reasoning. If she is a good judge, her decision, based on the tools and sources, will be reasonable and defensible, though there is still room for legitimate disagreement. (Supreme Court justices do not always agree about what is constitutional, and even the best judges' decisions are sometimes overturned on appeal.) The good judge can give strong reasons for thinking that precedent N is more central to the case before her than is statute M. Even though her reasons may not convince everyone, any good judge can see the force of her reasons.

The same is true of ethics. No simple rules will cover all cases. Just like the judge, the ethical person has to use her judgment. Of course, to be told "you must use your judgment" does not help much when you are not clear on what is to be judged, what factors must be weighed, and how to go about weighing those factors. Fortunately, the ethical person can draw on a variety of sources, such as specific rules, general principles, guiding ideas, values, and moral factors. The ethical person, when facing a difficult moral choice, must reason about which rules, values, principles, and so forth are relevant, analyze the problem in terms of those values and principles, and weigh the different factors in the light of guiding considerations.

Although experts generally agree about most of the ordinary, day-to-day ethical decisions engineers must make, they disagree about some cases. Ethical decisions are sometimes difficult. For example, although telling the truth is usually in the best interest of the company, in rare cases an engineer might have to choose between loyalty to his employer and telling the truth. Not every ethical person will make the same choice. However, an ethical person will make the decision reasonably, understanding the issues and principles involved, and be able to explain why he thinks that, in this particular case, the value of honesty is more important than loyalty to his employer (or vice versa).

These materials are meant to provide you with some of the tools, sources, and guiding considerations important to ethical decision making and to give you some general assistance in reasoning, analyzing, and weighing the factors involved in ethical decisions. They may not tell you what to do in every case, but they will help you to decide in an ethical, fair, and rational way, and they will help you to understand the reasons behind the ethical decisions that others make.

How to Use This Book

The materials in this volume present you with a variety of source materials and techniques to draw upon in making moral decisions. You will be given specific rules to be followed (for example, do not falsify tests or records), general principles that should be respected (for example, you should try to promote good consequences), values for which you should strive (for example, you should put a high priority on establishing and maintaining a partnership with nature), and factors and guiding ideas that influence the way these rules, principles, and values apply to particular situations (for example, one factor in weighing competing rules is that a rule that reflects an institutional duty has greater weight than a rule that does not. A guiding question in deciding whether a given solution is too risky is "Am I being a good trustee of the public safety?"). Sometimes the rules, values, and principles pull in opposite directions, and you will have to decide how to weigh them. Generally, specific rules have first priority. However, the specific rules are not arbitrary requirements. Rather, they are ways that engineers can put into practice the moral principles and values that apply to engineering. Rules, in other words, derive from the principles and values of engineering. Why, for example, is there is a specific rule that engineers must not violate the demands of safety? Because safety is a central value of engineering, and because acting unsafely usually violates the general principle that we should try to promote good consequences.

In some cases, following a specific rule might undermine rather than promote the value or principle on which the rule is based. When that happens, the rule has to be modified. People are not machines, and they should not blindly follow a rule regardless of the reason for that rule.

This complexity makes ethics both difficult and fascinating. There is no mechanical way of determining the right thing to do. So I have tried to give you as many tools as possible. For example, I suggest that in thinking about whether an engineering solution is sufficiently safe, you ask yourself, "Would I want my family to undergo this risk for this benefit?" Although this personal question often helps in thinking about safety, sometimes it provides no help at all, because you do not know whether you would want your family to take this risk. In that case, you must try something else. Use another factor or rule or value to reach a decision.

Because general moral understanding is as important as specific advice about tough issues, I have organized this book to facilitate understanding; to make clear the reasons for rules, values, and principles; to make clear why certain factors are important; and so forth. For example, one key moral idea in engineering ethics is that of community; so I have devoted one section to the idea of community. The idea of community gives rise to several different rules and values, which are discussed in that section. Another key moral concept is that of fairness (justice), and so another section is devoted to treating others fairly and well. The rules related to justice are discussed in that section. Thus, the actual rules, values, and guiding considerations are scattered throughout the volume. This approach makes it easier to understand the moral basis of the rules but harder to find and apply the rules. I have, therefore, summarized the major ideas in Appendix 2.

Ethics, like most things, requires practice. To help you practice making ethical decisions, I have included a fair number of cases. Some cases I discuss, while others I leave for you to think about and, perhaps, discuss with friends or colleagues. Generally, the cases are brief sketches of situations and do not include all possible relevant features. After all, ethical thinking often begins with asking yourself what else you need to know about a situation. A new piece of information may radically change your solution of an ethical problem. Normally, for example, you should not be a supplier of the company that employs you. Suppose, for example, you are both the owner of a small company that manufactures special coolants and a chemical engineer employed by the Z corporation, which manufactures vitamins. Generally, you should not sell coolants to the Z corporation. However, the fact that your company is the sole manufacturer of the only coolant that meets Z corporation's needs changes the situation dramatically. While you should avoid conflict of interest situations, you need not deny your employer a vital supply. Similarly, a relevant fact may make one of my recommendations inapplicable to your case.

It cannot be stressed enough that the recommendations made in this book are but the considered thoughts of one individual. No one has a monopoly on moral truth. This book is meant to be helpful to you in your thinking, not to replace your own moral judgment. You may think of other moral factors or principles not mentioned in these pages. You may disagree with some of the principles and recommendations. In ethics, as in almost everything, there is no substitute for your own, carefully considered judgment.

A Template for Moral Decision Making

One way to learn how to make good decisions is to look carefully at good examples of moral thinking, as in the discussion of Case 1. In analyzing the case, we started by listing our options, determining which steps we could take, and deciding how we might go about taking them. We then identified several relevant moral sources, such as the value of autonomy (the importance of letting people take charge of their own lives), the principle of fair dealing (making sure we hear Smith's side of things before taking action against him), and the principle of promoting good consequences (making sure our actions do not hurt Jones' career). We thought about how these sources apply to our problem. Then we gave reasons for weighing the different factors in this particular case. Finally, we reached a decision about what to do.

This is the general formula for ethical decision making. Sound ethical thinking requires two distinct components. To make sound ethical decisions, one has to have a good ethics toolkit, and one has to use those tools wisely in particular cases. In other words, you need to develop a general ethical framework you can bring to making decisions, and you have to analyze each case carefully as it arises.

Developing a general ethical framework involves developing an awareness of ethically sensitive situations (that is, knowledge of the issues) and developing a set of principles, values, rules, guiding ideals, and so forth that you can bring to the analysis of particular cases. This book can help with both of these tasks. It brings to your attention a large number of issues and ethically sensitive situations, some of which are obvious and some of which you may not have thought about. This book also provides you with a broad set of principles, values, rules, guiding ideals, and so forth. However, no book can cover everything: you may encounter situations I have not discussed or think of useful principles and values I have not mentioned. Moreover, you should not accept these recommendations blindly: you have a responsibility, as an ethical person, to ask yourself

about every sentence in this book, "Is thi
agree?" Developing an ethical framework
project. New experiences and the maturity ga
should continually prompt you to reexamine y ~~. .~~.~ ~~.~
values. Talk to others about ethical concerns, read other
books, and, above all, keep rethinking these questions as
carefully and critically as you can.

Having a good ethics framework does not help much if
you do not use it in making life decisions. Making
particular tough decisions can be thought of as a five-step
process:

Step 1. Clarify the moral decision to be made. What are your
options?
> What are the ethical issues involved? What choices do
> you have? Be creative in defining your options: often,
> the best option is not immediately obvious. As Sarah
> Merrill often remarks (in conversation), if, after
> analyzing your options, you feel ethically
> uncomfortable about all of them, you may need to be
> more creative when looking for possible solutions.

Step 2. Identify the moral considerations that are pertinent to the
particular situation you are thinking about. Which specific rules,
general principles, values, factors, and guiding ideas apply?
> Your general ethical framework should contain a large
> number of considerations, not all of which are relevant.
> Which ones are relevant to making this particular
> decision?

Step 3. Analyze the situation. How do the considerations
identified in step 2 apply to the situation? Which aspects of
the situation limit or modify the relevant rules, principles,
values, and factors?

Step 4. Determine how these moral considerations should be
weighed for this situation.

Step 4 is probably the most difficult. Does some aspect of the particular case suggest that, in making this particular decision, one factor or principle is more important or central than another?

Step 5. Calculate the result. What follows from steps 1 through 4? Which of the options listed in step 1 is best supported by the weighted considerations given in step 4? This tells you what to do.

As much as feasible, you want to accommodate all the moral considerations. What is the best compromise? Caroline Whitbeck suggests (in various unpublished papers) that ethical decision making is like design. When designing a car, one wants to achieve the best compromise between safety, reliability, economy, ease of use, looks, and so forth. Similarly, when making an ethical decision, one wants to achieve the best possible compromise between all the conflicting moral factors.

This five-step process is the standard procedure for dealing with a difficult moral decision. But you do not necessarily have to undertake this procedure every time you make an ethical decision. In some cases a different strategy may prove more useful. Ethical thinking is a craft, and a good craftsperson will use different techniques for different situations. Also, in many cases it is easy to know what is right, and we need no complicated decision-making process to determine what we should do. If a company rule clearly covers a situation, you must follow the rule, unless you have an overwhelming moral reason to do otherwise. Only in rare and special cases would the ethical engineer even consider breaking the law.[2] It is virtually never right for an engineer to lie in a professional context. Still, the ethical engineer must understand the process of ethical decision making, for two reasons. First, it is always good to know why something is the right thing to do, and second, in many situations it is not immediately clear what is right.

Sometimes constructing a specific flowchart helps in making the decision. Which flowchart proves most useful for a given decision depends upon the nature of the decision. The following flowchart sometimes helps in making ethical decisions.

Step 1. List options.
Step 2. See if any option is required; go to subroutine R1.
Step 3. Are any options marked "R"?

YES	NO
Check for conflict. Go to subroutine E1 for those conflicting options. Is any option marked both "X" and "R," or are two or more incompatible options marked "R"?	Go to subroutine E1 for all options. Eliminate all options marked "X." Is more than one option left?

YES	NO	YES	NO
Go to subroutine C1. Proceed to step 4.	*Decision!* Select the option. End.	Proceed to step 4.	*Decision!* Select the option. End.

Step 4. Consult values and principles.

We are now at the point at which the rules do not help us. All we can do is ask ourselves which values and principles tell against each remaining option and which values and principles speak in favor of each remaining option. Then we must weigh these values and principles in the light of relevant factors and guiding ideas, to try to make the best choice possible.

Decision!
Select the option.
End.

Subroutine R1

For each option: does any specific rule require selecting the option?

	YES	NO
	Does following the specific rule violate a general principle or value?	Next option.

YES	NO
Does the value or principle justify breaking the rule in this case?	Mark the option "R." Next option.

YES	NO
Next option.	Mark the option "R." Next option.

Return.

Subroutine E1

For each option:

Step 1. Does the option violate a specific rule?

YES	NO
Does following the specific rule in this case violate a general principle?	Next option.

YES	NO
Is the general principle sufficiently important in this case to justify breaking the specific rule? (See Chapter 4, "When to Break the Rules.")	Place a question mark under the option. Proceed to step 2.

YES	NO
Next option.	Place a question mark under the option. Proceed to step 2.

Step 2. Does following the specific rule in this case violate a value?

YES	NO
Is the value sufficiently important in this case to justify breaking the specific rule?	Mark the option "X." Next option.

YES	NO
Next option.	Put a question mark under the option. If there are two question marks under the option, mark the option "X." Next option.

Return.

Subroutine C1

You have a moral dilemma: one rule requires an action that conflicts with another rule. You must resolve the dilemma.

Step 1. Is there a way to modify the option so it still follows one rule without violating the other? If so, restart the procedure with the new option. If not, go to step 2.

Step 2. Consider the relative importance of the two rules and the extent to which the act violates the rule. Do any values, principles, factors, or guiding ideas mitigate or strengthen the force of either of the two rules in this case? (For example, if the rule requiring an option is an institutional duty, and the rule forbidding the action is not an institutional duty, this suggests one should perform the action.) How direct is your responsibility in this case? How much harm would be caused in each case? This series of questions can be developed only on a case-by-case basis.

Step 3. Is there a clear preference?

YES	NO
Decision! Select that option. End.	Eliminate all options not marked "R." Return.

Only rarely will you need to go through such an elaborate procedure, but most moral thinking uses some simplified version of the decision-making strategies elaborated above.

Part 2 furnishes you with tools and sources for making ethical decisions. I have frequently illustrated these materials with cases and examples. Further and more comprehensive applications of these tools and sources to specific issues and problems in engineering ethics come in Part 3. Together, they are meant to give you a good foundation in ethical engineering.

PART TWO

Sources of Ethical Decision Making

3

Values of the Engineering Profession

Moral thinking consists of using reason-guided judgment to make particular decisions by drawing upon moral sources, factors, and guiding ideas. Part 2 provides you with many of the tools you will need to make ethical decisions and illustrates these tools with cases and examples. Part 2 also deals with some of the important issues in engineering ethics, such as product safety, and prepares you to think about the further issues, such as whistleblowing, that are discussed in Part 3.

One important source engineers may draw upon in making ethical decisions is the set of values central to engineering as a profession. Engineering, after all, is not just a way of making a living. It is a profession, a "calling," in which individuals are personally committed to using their skills and abilities to achieve a high social goal. If you see engineering as "just a job," you will not obtain the satisfaction and sense of purpose that engineering offers,[1] and you will not be an ethical engineer. By contrast, you will be a better and happier engineer if you see your work as dedicated to a worthwhile ideal, just as the best and happiest physicians are those devoted to healing and to the ideal of health. Engineering is not just a way of making a buck—it is also a moral commitment.

What makes engineering so important? Many different types of engineers exist, and each serves society in a different way. Nonetheless, every engineer, no matter how small or big his or her job, helps to expand the frontiers of human knowledge and create a better life. Philosophers as diverse as John Locke and Karl Marx have argued that we are by nature creative producers: the distinctive human attribute is the ability to reshape the world in line with our dreams and visions. Other animals make things; ants build mounds and beavers build dams. But beavers never hold conferences on building better dams. Human beings, unlike beavers and ants, can envision a novel future that better reflects our values, and we can remake the world in accordance with that vision. If this is indeed the essential human characteristic, then engineering is the essential human science. Engineers, after all, give shape to dreams: they are the sculptors of society, for together, in the countless projects completed in companies and firms throughout the world, they determine the shape of the world in which we all live.

What ties engineers together into a profession is not just that engineers make things, but that they make things in a special way we might call "the engineering way." Engineers do not guess haphazardly or sloppily: the engineering way is precise, rational, and careful. Engineers do not take wild risks: the engineering way is to be responsible about safety. While painters tend to be solitary, each working alone on his own painting, the engineering way is to work as a team. More generally, engineering is the science of technology, and technology is practical wisdom.[2] Because reflecting on such theoretical matters as human nature and the nature of technology can help us in making particular tough decisions, it is worth taking a moment to think about the nature of technology. What does it mean to say that technology is practical wisdom? Practical wisdom is engaging wisely in the enterprise of building a human world, a world that reflects human nature. Moreover, as Aristotle pointed out, wisdom is the habit of acting in ways that lead to excellence in expressing our nature. So if technology is practical wisdom, then technology reflects human nature. Three examples will help explain this point.

First, again citing Aristotle, we are rational animals. And so technology must reflect both our being rational and our being animal. Because we are animals, we are part of nature, part of the beauty and wonder of the natural world. Because we are rational, because we have visions and standards, we must shape our lives and our world. These two sides of human nature mean that we must live in partnership with nature. We should be neither passive nor oblivious to the natural characteristics of the world as we find it. Just as the good woodworker respects and works with the individual characteristics of wood, its particular grain and color, while shaping it into a box or chair that serves human needs and expresses a sense of beauty, so the good engineer respects the peculiar beauties of nature while reshaping the world in a way that is conducive to human welfare, rationally conceived. We must wisely balance our visions (being rational) with nature (being an animal).

Second, because we are *rational* animals, we should reshape the world rationally: technology requires the thoughtful and innovate use of precise, clearly articulated knowledge. Third, because it is our nature, as Aristotle says, to be social animals, technology is a community activity in two ways: technology is conducted communally, and it takes account of the communal character of human welfare.

These ruminations on technology as practical wisdom have some important consequences. For example, it follows that technology is not value-neutral. Technology is not the ability to manipulate the environment as such but is instead the search for human excellence. Moreover, technology is committed, by its very nature, to community, to rationality, and to partnership with nature. So technology is value-laden both in its defining goal and in its defining methods. We can put all these ideas together in a one-sentence definition of engineering:

Engineering is the safe advancement of the progress of the human community, in partnership with nature, through know-how used in a systematic practice of clear, clean, practical decision-making.[3]

If this definition correctly describes the essence of engineering as a profession, then engineering, by its nature, is dedicated to five key values: (1) safety, (2) human progress, (3) clean, clear decision making, (4) community, and (5) partnership with nature. These values play an important role in the making of ethical decisions.

But the values of engineering extend beyond the workplace. Engineering is not only a job but a way of life. The ethical engineer's commitment to safety does not end when she pulls out of the parking lot at the end of the day: she retains her concern for safety while playing golf, shopping, skiing, going to the opera, and building furniture in her workshop. Of course, each of us is different, and we all have limits. No one can expect every engineer to give full weight to every value in his or her off-hours. Nevertheless, each engineer should strive to come as close to the "ideal" engineer as possible. So it is useful to talk about an ideal or model engineer, "the compleat engineer," who not only makes correct ethical decisions but instantiates all the ideals of engineering as a profession.

Safety

Engineering as a profession is committed to safety, as every engineer knows. But what exactly is safety, and how safe is safe enough?[4]

Safety does not mean the absence of all risk. Risk is a necessary concomitant of progress, indeed, of life itself. Some risks are worthwhile because of the benefits obtained by taking the risk. For example, as a society, we accept 55,000 deaths a year as the price of the convenience of the automobile.[5] The value of safety does not require that engineers must sacrifice everything else to eliminate the risk of a single life being lost, and so engineers need not demand an end to the manufacture of automobiles.[6] If we were willing to spend $100,000 on safety devices for each car, we could make cars much safer than they are. This would mean, of course, that very few people could afford to drive. The value of safety does not require automotive engineers to design cars that almost no one can afford.

In short, every risk must be balanced against the benefits of the product or process.

Extent of a Risk

Three factors determine the extent of a risk:

1. How severe is the possible harm to each individual?
2. How widespread is the danger?
3. How likely is the danger?

The greater the risk, the more imperative it is that the company reveal the risk fully and promptly. The degree of risk depends on the three related factors listed above.

Factor 3 concerns the likelihood of harm. Each risk has a threshold of significance. If there is only one chance in a million that an accident might harm a few people, that likelihood is below the threshold of significance (it is orders of magnitude below the general death rate). By contrast, a one-in-a-million chance of a major catastrophe, such as nuclear war, is a significant risk because of the scale of the catastrophe. In general, the higher the stakes, the lower the threshold of significance. Once the threshold of significance is passed, the obligation to publicize the risk increases with the likelihood of harm resulting.

Factors 1 and 2 concern the distribution of risk. A million-dollar risk to one person is more troublesome than a one-dollar risk to a million people. Of first importance is devastating harm to an individual, such as death or severe bodily injury. If a company's proposed action poses a significantly likely possibility of devastating harm, then only very strong reasons (such as an imperative need for national security) justify keeping the risk secret. The importance of widespread risks depends upon two factors: the average possible harm and the total possible harm. For example, a one-dollar harm to a million people is a low average harm (one dollar) but a high total harm (a million dollars). A total harm of a million dollars may be a significant loss for a community because of its cumulative affect on commerce and government revenues. Obviously, a small, poor community will be more affected by a given total loss than will a large, wealthy community, so the total harm must be assessed in the context of the particular community and its ability to withstand such a loss. Both average and total harm must be considered: the greater the average and the total harm, the greater the company's obligation to avoid or publicize the risk.

Balancing Risks against Benefits

Of course, the engineer would prefer to take no risks at all. Unfortunately, this is not feasible. So the engineer must decide whether the benefit is worth the risk involved. There is no simple way to make this decision. However, a few factors are worth mentioning. These factors may not help decide all cases, but often at least one will be useful in thinking about a particular risk.

First, when weighing risks against benefits, the responsible engineer places a high value on minimizing risk: she seeks the lowest value of likelihood of harm multiplied by total possible harm. The responsible designer of automobiles goes to considerable lengths to make automobile travel as safe as feasible, even if that means higher costs or requires compromises in style and image. When in doubt, be conservative.

Second, a rough but useful test an engineer may use is to ask, "Would I be willing to have my family undergo this risk for these benefits?"

Third, safety costs more in the short term but saves money in the long run. As a rule, the more reliable a machine is, the higher the cost to make it, though more reliable machines save money in downtime and repairs. The same is true of safety. The initial or primary costs of a safer product or process tend to be higher. More risky products and processes, however, tend to have higher long-term or secondary costs, such as liability costs (lawsuits and fines), recall costs, lost sales because of unfavorable publicity, and time lost when the product or process has to be modified. As Mike Martin and Roland Schinzinger point out, the low primary costs of high-risk products and processes must be balanced against the high secondary costs, and the high primary costs of low-risk products must be balanced against the low secondary costs. Minimal total cost to the manufacturer is thus secured somewhere in the middle of the safety scale, at a point M where "incremental savings in primary cost . . . are offset by an equal incremental increase in secondary cost."[7] Although point M is ideal from a purely financial point of view, the ethical engineer has a tendency to opt for solutions somewhat less risky than M.

A fourth guideline comes from the fact that an engineer is a trustee of the public welfare and should act like the administrator of a trust fund or the conservator of an estate. A trustee does not perform his task well if he is so averse to taking risks that the fund he manages does overwhelmingly worse than the market average; nevertheless, he ought to be more cautious than the average investor, since his primary directive is to protect (preserve) the fund or estate. Thus, the engineer should exercise slightly more caution on the behalf of others than he would exercise for himself.

Nature of Risks

The extent of the risk is not the only factor to be weighed against the benefit: the nature of the risk is also important. For example, those who use automobiles are aware of the risks and the benefits and have some choice in the matter. Drivers and passengers voluntarily take the risk. Furthermore, the same people who take the risk also receive the benefit. There is a big difference between my voluntarily taking a risk to get something I want and your putting me at risk, without my knowledge or consent, to obtain something you want. So engineers have a special reason to avoid imposing risks on the unwary, or on those who have no choice, or on those who receive no benefit from the risk.[8]

This difference between risks suggests three key factors in assessing acceptable risks:

1. Is the risk voluntarily taken?
2. Do those at risk know the potential risks?
3. Do those at risk reap the benefits of the risk?

These factors prove useful in three ways. First, when the engineer has to choose between two risks, she will prefer (other things being equal) a voluntary to an involuntary risk, and she will prefer a risk borne by those who benefit to one borne by those who do not. For example, in a nuclear power plant, a risk to workers is, other things being equal, more acceptable than a risk to residents, since workers have more choice than residents and workers receive more of the benefits of the plant than do residents. So the three factors listed above help us decide which risk to take when we have a choice. Second, the factors help in deciding whether to impose a particular risk. A given risk is worse to the extent that it is involuntary, to the extent that those at risk do not know the risk, and to the extent that those taking the risk do not benefit. So the three factors help us to determine how bad a given risk is. Third, these factors make clear the importance of publicizing risks.

Publicizing Risks

Since risks that are voluntarily taken are better than involuntary ones, it might seem that companies should always publicize every risk its operations pose to the public. This standard is too stringent, however. Newspapers looking for stories that sell papers are likely to give undue attention to very remote risks. Public fanfare about a remote risk serves neither the public nor the company. Moreover, publicizing a risk may compromise trade secrets. So, although the default value is to publicize, there are times when a company need not advertise a risk.

In determining when and whether to publicize a risk posed by a contemplated company action, the engineer or executive should ask herself five key questions:

1. Do I have a legal duty to publicize the risk? This question takes priority over the other three. A company must meet its legal obligations. If there is no legal duty to publicize the risk, the executive or engineer should consider the next three questions.

2. Can the community take action to reduce the risk?
Depending on the nature of the risk, the community may choose from a wide range of options designed to mitigate or guard against the risk posed by the company's or firm's activities. To give but a few examples, the community might make emergency preparations (such as formulating an evacuation plan and instituting periodic evacuation drills, arranging for extra fire-fighting assistance in case of an industrial accident, installing extra water mains in the vicinity of the plant, and giving special training to local emergency crews), construct retaining walls, alter flood planning and management, institute periodic state inspections, oversee construction, impose restrictions on plant operations, or even relocate homeowners.

When such options are feasible and significantly lower the risk of potential harm, the community must be given the opportunity to decide whether implementing one or more of these options is warranted. This decision cannot be made intelligently if the community does not fully understand the nature of the risk. Thus, when the community could take feasible and appropriate measures, the company or firm has a duty to inform the community of the risk and to cooperate with the community in exploring options early enough that the community can make intelligent decisions. Thus, how far in advance of implementation the company must publicize the risk depends on the nature of the community action available. A simple retaining wall can be built quickly, while altering complex flood plans requires considerably more time for study, pricing, legislative action, and construction of facilities such as dams.[9]

3. How great is the risk? For example, because the risks posed by nuclear power plants tend to be severe and widespread, it is imperative that any risks posed by a nuclear power plant to either workers or residents be well publicized rather than hidden or downplayed.

4. Are there legitimate reasons for withholding the information? National security, genuine business and trade secrets, and preventing panic are legitimate factors that tell in favor of not publicizing a risk. These factors must be balanced against the first three.

5. How much will the company be hurt by publicizing the risk? Firms and companies must balance public stewardship against the economic facts of survival. At one extreme, a firm or company must be prepared to go out of business rather than pose a significant risk of world disaster. At the other extreme, a company need not publicize a trivial risk if publicizing the risk would destroy the company. Most cases lie between these extremes. Because innovation is the soul of engineering, the company must do its best to find ways of publicizing the risk that minimize damage to the company. For example, the company can propose community action to minimize risk at the time it publicizes the risk, thus helping the community protect itself in ways that do not hurt the company.

In sum, the ethical engineer places a high value on avoiding risks and on publicizing those that are worth taking.

The value placed by engineers on safety extends beyond the workplace. Valuing safety also means placing a premium on health as well as avoiding accidents and committing oneself to due care in all things. So the compleat engineer will not drive recklessly, will not drive an unsafe car, will not leave tools lying about where others may trip over them, will maintain a healthy diet, and so forth.

Illustrating Cases and Examples

Case 2: Large doses of N have been shown to cause cancer in laboratory rats. In addition, studies show that workers who have had long-term exposure to N exhibit a significantly higher than average rate of cancer. Using N in a lipstick under study by your company would give that lipstick a slightly brighter color than any lipstick now on the market. Is it ethical to use N in a lipstick?

Discussion: The fact that large doses of N cause cancer in rats does not mean that N will cause cancer to human beings when applied to the lips in small quantities: human beings differ from rats, large doses differ from small doses, and application to the lips differs from injection or ingestion. Nevertheless, if the company uses N in a lipstick, the customers—unlike the rats in the study—would be subject to long-term exposure. For these reasons, it is difficult to assess the likelihood of the risk. Clearly, however, the risk would be both severe and widespread. In sum, the lab results suggest a significant possibility of harm to customers. Yet a significant possibility is not the same as a certainty. We must balance the benefits of using N in a lipstick against the risks. To a large extent, this process involves guesswork, since we do not know how likely the risk is. Fortunately, we are all used to operating under uncertainty. When you choose between two films for your Saturday night outing, you do not know which film would be more enjoyable or worthwhile. It could even be that neither film is worth the time or money. You make the best decision you can, taking into consideration any relevant factors (such as reviews, a friend's recommendations, and how much attending the film will cost).

In this case, the value of safety suggests that N should not be used in a commercial lipstick. A slightly brighter lipstick provides only slight benefits to human welfare. In addition, many satisfying lipsticks are already on the market, and no one's health and happiness depends on how bright her lipstick is. However, the risk and likely suffering (setback of human welfare) are significant. You would not, after all, want your daughter or mother to risk getting cancer merely to have slightly brighter lipstick. Moreover, while the benefit does go to those at risk, buyers of the lipstick are unlikely to be fully aware of the risk. Clearly, the potential costs of lawsuits and the decreased sales of all the company's products as a result of adverse publicity make selling a lipstick using N economically unwise (point M falls on the side of forbearance). And an engineer who used N in a lipstick would not be acting as a faithful trustee of the public welfare. Thus, using N in a commercial lipstick would violate the engineer's commitment to safety. In addition, the strong possibility of producing a significant number of carcinomas clearly sets back human welfare more than the slight advantage of a brighter lipstick advances it. So using N in the lipstick violates the engineer's commitment to advancing human welfare. (See also "The Duty to Leave the World No Worse" in Chapter 4.)

Notice what we have done so far. We began with somewhat theoretical conceptions of human nature and of technology as practical wisdom. We then derived as a consequence a definition of engineering from which we extracted a value—safety. We developed some guiding ideas in applying that value and used our guidelines to decide an actual case. This illustrates the kind of ethical thinking that lies at the heart of sound decision making.

Case 3: Drug P shows some promise of lengthening the lives of late-stage AIDS patients. However, laboratory tests indicate that P may cause liver cancer and ulcers. Is it ethical to market P?

Discussion: Drug P is a worthwhile risk. First, since P would be a prescription drug, AIDS patients can be informed of the possible dangers of P and would have a choice about whether to take the drug. Thus, the risk would be known and voluntarily borne by those who would receive the benefit. Moreover, it is not irrational for a late-stage AIDS patient, who may not live very long without P, to choose to take the risk of developing ulcers and liver cancer some years later. If a member of your family were a late-stage AIDS patient, you would want her to have the choice of taking P. Finally, marketing P may also advance human knowledge and is more likely to advance human welfare than to cause suffering. So the value of safety is not compromised by marketing P, and the commitment to human progress suggests that one should market P.

Case 4: On January 4, 1987, 16 people died and 170 were injured when an Amtrak passenger train traveling at 128 mph collided with a Conrail freight train traveling about 60 mph. The speed limits for the two trains are 103 and 30 mph, respectively. (Commercial pressure to keep on schedule encourages speeding.) The blood and urine of the

Conrail train's engineer tested positive for marijuana. He had previously had his driver's license suspended and had been indicted for drunk driving. Amtrak trains have automatic brakes that are designed to slow a speeding train, while the Conrail train did not. The radio on the Conrail train was broken and had been temporarily replaced with a hand-held radio. The whistle that was supposed to serve as a warning had been taped over. The Federal Railroad Commission discovered seventy-five other trains with taped whistles. Separate tracks for freight and passenger trains are considered too expensive.[10]

Case 5: In September of 1968 tests were begun on a new type of contraceptive device, the Dalkon Shield.[11] By the summer of 1969, 640 women had been tested. The Dalkon Shield showed a pregnancy rate of 1.1 percent, as low as or lower than that of birth control pills. By June of 1970, the shield was being marketed on a small scale. Several changes had been made to the shield after the tests were run, making it thinner and more flexible. Moreover, copper had been added to the shield. The A. H. Robins Corporation knew that changes had been made after testing and also knew that the actual pregnancy rate in the original study had been questioned. (For example, Jack Freund, vice-president of Robins' medical department, expressed concern that the studies had not been conducted long enough; he said he had been told that the actual pregnancy rate, with a follow-up period, had been 2.3 percent.) Nonetheless, Robins decided to purchase rights to the device on June 12. Two weeks later, Robins became aware that the tail of the device might wick material containing infectious material into the uterus. In July, the company made further changes to the width of the device and changed the shape of the legs to teardrops. The company did not test these changes (though Robins later claimed to have consulted experts and also claimed that "there is no evidence that these changes affected the safety of the Shield"). Evidence of septic abortions caused by the shield, effectiveness rates below those of the pill, deteriorating shields, and problems continued to mount. Many shield users filed lawsuits against the company. Eventually, on June 28, 1974, two days after a letter from the Food and Drug Administration (FDA) recommended removal, Robins removed the shield from the market. However, the company did not issue a formal recall and claimed in a press release that "performance has clearly been satisfactory."

Case 6: The FDA ran a series of tests in which Narbitol, an emulsifier used in certain foods, produced mutations in laboratory animals. The FDA required that a warning be printed on the labels of all food products containing Narbitol. This requirement does not apply to imported foods. A significant part of your company's sales come from Dark Dreams, an expensive chocolate sauce containing Narbitol. Marketing research indicates that a warning would seriously dampen sales of Dark Dreams. You have several options: (1) discontinue producing Dark Dreams until a safer emulsifier can feasibly be used, which will take considerable time and research because the most commonly used safe emulsifiers are incompatible with Dark Dreams, causing clotting and discoloration; (2) use another emulsifier, Starbitol, about which no FDA regulation as yet exists, but which early evidence shows likely to be carcinogenic; (3) sell Dark Dreams through foreign import markets, thereby circumventing the FDA order; or (4) sell Dark Dreams with the warning label.

Human Progress

Human progress has two basic components: knowledge and welfare (improving the lives of fellow human beings both materially and psychologically). The ethical engineer is dedicated to the advancement of knowledge, both practical and theoretical. This means that the compleat engineer is drawn to innovative solutions that advance human knowledge. He keeps up with his field, always eager to learn new techniques and approaches. He is intellectually curious and loves to learn about all sorts of things. And he seeks appropriate means of sharing his knowledge (in ways that do not compromise his loyalty to his company). The ethical engineer is also dedicated to the advancement of human welfare. He wants to make people's lives better. This means that he seeks to use technology to help others rather than to hurt them. In his work, he is mindful of the human costs and potential benefits of engineering and employment decisions. In general, the compleat engineer is civic-minded, showing compassion and being helpful to others. He may volunteer his services for community and charitable projects, acquaint himself with social problems such as world hunger and future energy needs, and speak out publicly on those issues about which he has special knowledge. Kindness to a lost child or stranger, helping a neighbor with a problem, giving to charity, and writing a letter to the editor about nuclear energy are all ways in which the compleat engineer might express his commitment to human progress.

Clean, Clear Decision Making

People make decisions in many ways. Engineering as a profession is dedicated to making decisions by clean, clear, rigorous thinking. The engineer analyzes the problem; gathers and records precise and reliable information; uses care, concentration, and ingenuity in solving the problem; and tests his solution to achieve excellence. Sloppy, haphazard, vague, and half-baked thinking are contrary to "the engineering way."[12] So the engineer is dedicated to such values as

precision
clarity
ingenuity and creativity
concentration and care
the value of excellence generally

In the workplace, this means meticulous precision and concentration, careful and accurate record keeping, and striving for excellence in all facets of one's work. The ethical engineer welcomes new ideas and creativity,[13] though always striving to make innovations precise and safe.

Outside of work, the compleat engineer has an appreciation of fine craft and excellence, in areas as diverse as poetry writing, woodworking, teaching, and clock repairing. The compleat engineer prefers neatness of dress and speech to lazy, vague, ungrammatical speech and a slovenly appearance. She attempts to be fair and precise in all things, including personal relationships and decisions about which car to purchase. The compleat engineer does not vote for a candidate because of how he looks on television but on the basis of careful and rigorous attention to the facts and issues. She keeps accurate income tax records and is meticulous about her personal finances, paying her bills on time, balancing her checkbook, and so forth.

Community

Community is a central value in engineering ethics. Cooperation between engineers is essential, of course, but the term *community* denotes much more than sharing information and ideas with colleagues and coworkers.

A community is a group of persons working out a joint moral vision through common institutions, practices, relationships, and shared experiences, all of which are dedicated to that vision. Perhaps the clearest example would be a small space colony, in which everyone sees himself as a partner in a common project. Each person plays a well-defined role in this project, whether as gardener or science officer, and each is committed to the others' success and welfare in this remote region of space. The value of their enterprise, as well as its precariousness, gives each member of the colony a sense of self-worth and leads each to view his teammates with respect and concern.

It is important to employers and employees alike that the workplace be a community of this sort.

Being part of a community is important to the individual engineer because it makes her a happier and better engineer. Most people spend a third of their waking lives at work and derive a good part of their self-esteem and sense of who they are from their jobs. An engineer's life will be enormously more pleasant and rewarding if she sees herself as part of a worthwhile and socially important project. Not only does this give her life as a whole a sense of meaning, but it also makes rewarding what might otherwise be less interesting tasks. Thus, each engineer needs to understand the way in which her contribution fits into the bigger picture and must have a sense of the importance and value of the larger project of which her work is a part. In addition, people enjoy going to work if the workplace is supportive, caring, and demanding in ways that make sense. All people need to feel that they belong somewhere, that they are valued, and that they are among friends. If engineers feel that the company is fair and cares about them, that their colleagues are out to help them rather than stab them in the back, and that they can trust others in the workplace to be moral and sincere, then they will love their work. If, by contrast, engineers feel that the company is just using them, that their colleagues are deceitful, cruel, or underhanded, and that they have to look out for themselves instead of concentrating on their work, then they will be unhappy and will not flourish and develop as engineers. If the workplace has a community atmosphere, engineers will be highly motivated and will reach their personal best in skill and performance. A good workplace makes for a good and a happy engineer.

These same facts make a community atmosphere attractive to an employer. Engineers who are part of a community make better employees. If the company is loyal to its employees, treats them fairly and supportively, and makes them feel valued, then the employees will give their best to the company. Loyalty begets loyalty, and a company has no greater asset than the loyalty, skills, and motivation of its employees. By contrast, a company that deceives its employees can expect dishonesty in return. If the company is not ethical, neither will its employees be ethical. Stealing, featherbedding, fudging, coasting, attrition, and ignoring the company's interests are rare practices in companies that truly function as a community.

This fact must be kept firmly in mind, because often both employees and employers can achieve short-term goals by violating the demands of community. So it is tempting to gain a short-term advantage by lying, exploiting, and adopting other unethical practices. But if you do this, you will pay for it in the long run. Fear is an effective short-term motivator of employees but a poor long-term motivator. You may get a promotion by lying or fudging, but, in the long run, you will make coming to work miserable. It is worthwhile to make short-term sacrifices or to give up an opportunity for the sake of community. In the long run, everyone benefits.

The so-called prisoner's dilemma provides an interesting illustration of this point. Two prisoners, A and B, are told that if no one confesses, each will get two years in jail. If one confesses and the other does not, the one who confesses will be sentenced to one year in jail, while the other will be sentenced to ten years. If both confess, both will spend six years in jail. Clearly, they should both refuse to confess. In a community atmosphere, where people see themselves as part of a team, neither will confess. But in a self-seeking atmosphere, each prisoner will confess because he cannot trust the other not to try to get an advantage for himself. Thus, in a self-seeking atmosphere, both lose; while in a community atmosphere, both gain. Of course, the prisoner's dilemma is an artificial situation, but it is important because many real-life situations have the same logic as the prisoner's dilemma.

The compleat engineer views her job, her family, her town, her country, and humanity as a whole as a community of this sort. She does her part in the human enterprise, takes pleasure in the success of others, and feels a sense of kinship with all human beings.

Thinking of a company as a community affects the way companies operate. A company that operates as a community will not overcompartmentalize its processes, with the result that each group does not know what the other is doing. For example, if design and manufacture are completely separated, manufacturing engineers will not feel a strong sense of being teammates with design engineers. This not only impairs the attitudes of engineers, but also hurts efficiency:

> We learned this lesson at Hewlett-Packard a decade ago. . . . Our manufacturing engineers used to play a somewhat passive role in the innovation process. They assumed that whatever the design engineers threw over the fence, manufacturing would build. Today, manufacturing engineers are part of the product design team from day one of a project. . . . The collaboration between R&D and manufacturing has changed both functions for the better. . . . In order to make day-to-day adaptations and mid-course corrections in production, there must be continual communication between engineers and workers and between the design and manufacturing arms of the company.[14]

Illustrating Case

Case 7: You and Smith are the two major candidates for a promotion to become the head of department N. Smith's chances for the promotion depend largely, you think, upon the outcome of the project he is now directing. You can "sandbag" Smith's project by asking a superior to reassign some of the key people in Smith's project to your project, although you do not really need any more help. Should you do it?

Discussion: To do this would violate the value of community. You would be seeking your own advantage in an unfair way that would hurt the company. You might benefit in the short run, but in the long run this kind of underhanded back stabbing hurts both you and the company. If you indulge in this kind of behavior, others will treat you the same way, and you cannot expect the company or coworkers to be loyal to you. Do you really want to work in a place in which other people treat you this way? (In addition, to the extent that Smith's project would advance human progress, you are setting back rather than promoting human knowledge and welfare.)

Partnership with Nature

As noted earlier, the essence of being human is our urge and ability to build and make things that change the environment in which we live.[15] Thus, engineering is the distinctively human science. And the way engineers regard their task has profound moral significance. Engineering is the way we relate to the world in which we find ourselves, and how we do this defines our role in the cosmos. Engineering, in other words, is one way to answer the question "What is human?"

This is why partnership with nature is a crucial part of

engineering as a calling. Human beings are rational animals, and we are untrue to ourselves if we deny either the "rational" or the "animal."

Environmental Awareness

Environmental awareness has two aspects. The first concerns direct harm to the quality of human life. This may be called "environmentalism as prudence." For example, we have to be concerned about the effect on the ozone layer of chlorofluorocarbons, which take twenty to fifty years to reach the ozone layer (so that if we stopped using chlorofluorocarbons today, we would still experience at least twenty years of further damage to the ozone layer). Ozone in the upper atmosphere absorbs and converts to heat and chemical energy a substantial portion of the ultraviolet-B radiation emitted by the sun. Ultraviolet-B radiation damages DNA, harms agricultural crops, and affects phytoplankton (the keystone of the ocean's food chain). Cataracts and melanoma (a potentially lethal form of skin cancer) increase with exposure to ultraviolet radiation, especially among lighter-skinned peoples. Some studies suggest that ultraviolet-B weakens the immune systems of a variety of animals, including human beings. Ironically, erosion of the ozone in the upper atmosphere could increase ground-level ozone. The ensuing smog would stunt the growth of plants and create respiratory distress.

A second example is the Aral Sea project. The Soviet Union began a giant engineering project in the 1960s to take water from the Aral Sea to make the arid regions around it arable. The project proved a disaster: changing the riverbed patterns resulted in an irreversible drying of the once-scenic Aral (which was so lovely there were at one time plans to make it the "Russian Riviera"). As the Aral dried out, vast salt fields were left behind. The wind scattered the salt, making the land unfit for farming. As a result, thriving villages have become ghost towns, and a scenic region has become an ugly moonscape.[16]

As another example, while controversy still erupts over the extent of the problem of acid rain, evidence suggests that acid raid might have severe adverse consequences. Acid rain can occur naturally, but burning coal or gasoline may produce SO_2, which becomes SO_3 in the air and then joins with water droplets to form H_2SO_4, or sulfuric acid. Natural rainfall (unaffected by acid rain) has a pH of 5.6. A survey of 1,500 lakes in Norway showed that 70 percent of the lakes with a pH below 4.3 contain no fish. Some lakes and streams in the Adirondack mountains in New York showed a pH of 4.2 to 4.5. A rainfall with a pH of 2.4 (the equivalent of vinegar) was reported in 1974 in Scotland.[17]

Finally, environmental issues such as groundwater contamination directly affect human health and welfare. From October 1986 to September 1987, the National Wildlife Federation found over 100,000 violations of federal public health standards for drinking water, affecting 40 million people. In 94 percent of these cases the public was not notified. The Environmental Protection Agency reports that seventy-four different pesticides were found in the groundwater of thirty-five states.[18]

The second aspect of environmentalism concerns the preservation of nature for its own sake. This may be called "environmentalism as an ethic." This second aspect requires an understanding of our own place in the natural world.

One view about our place in nature is called the Gaia theory.[19] According to the Gaia theory, we should understand the entire earth as if it were a single organism. More precisely, the theory claims that through complex mutual interactions between the biosphere and the geophysical realm, the earth maintains itself much as a living organism does. In short, the earth is a homeostatic system. Although much that has been written about the Gaia theory is premature or even silly, the theory says nothing particularly mystical, if properly understood. For example, it assumes "no plan or intention" and ascribes to the earth "no 'soul' or other mystical power."[20] The mechanisms it describes are purely physical. For example, "dormant microbes . . . come out of their spore states and remove gas from the atmosphere when conditions are right, as though they were built-in safety mechanisms for correcting environmental imbalances."[21]

The Gaia theory has several important consequences. First, the "climatic system is in many ways more robust and resilient than has been generally believed."[22] Nevertheless, this resiliency depends on biological diversity, and so it is crucial to the health of the planet as a whole to maintain biological diversity. Thus, Gaia theorists are disturbed by large-scale agriculture, which produces massive destruction of forests, wild lands, natural shelters, and windbreaks; pollutes the watershed; erodes the soil; and replaces a highly diverse field or forest with acres devoted to cultivating a single plant species. In short, problems such as the greenhouse effect, depletion of the ozone layer, and acid rain are not necessarily catastrophic, so long as we leave intact the earth's mechanisms for dealing with such imbalances. However, since natural mechanisms can take thousands of years, "to count on the biota collectively to restore comfortable conditions is . . . foolhardy."[23] What the Gaia theory counsels, then, is a balanced strategy of minimizing environmental deterioration while maintaining diversity in the biosphere.

Other writers suggest that trees and other natural objects have "rights."[24] I would argue, however, that natural objects do not have rights, because to have rights a thing must have interests, and to have interests a thing must have a worldview, that is, standards or values in terms of which it measures some futures preferable to others. To have interests, a thing has to have rudimentary goals and commitments. By contrast, whatever happens to the Grand Canyon is all the canyon could ask for. If there were never any sentient creatures in the world, if the universe were forever empty of thinking, feeling organisms, if there were nothing to see the Grand Canyon, then it would not much matter whether there was a Grand Canyon in Arizona or a mudflat. So the Grand Canyon has no rights. Only people and, to a lesser extent, animals have rights.

But with rights come obligations, and people do have obligations to the natural world. Human beings have a two-sided nature: we are animals that create. We reshape nature to our vision, but we are a part of that nature. We are thus true to our nature only if we are good partners with nature, working with nature in fulfilling our dreams.[25]

I suggest, then, that we are neither lords nor caretakers of the planet but instead partners with the planet. A partnership involves mutual growth. This means respecting nature even as we change the face of the globe. If trees have rights, it is wrong to cut down any trees. If we have no obligation toward nature, we could cut down all the trees if we choose. If I am right, we may log selectively, preserving some virgin forests intact, clear-cutting some selected areas (though we have already done too much of that), and partially harvesting other regions in ways that minimize damage to the ecosystem. It is not acceptable, however, to cut down all the hardwoods and replace them with fast-growing pine, as some logging companies do, for this diminishes the diversity of nature.

Establishing a partnership with nature has no simple rules. It is difficult even to be clear about what "nature" and "natural" mean. In one sense, since we are a part of nature, everything we do is "natural": ants and human beings are both animals, and so what we make is as much a part of nature as an anthill.[26] Bridge builders and beavers obey the same laws of physics. In this sense, human processes are also natural processes. Perhaps some people mean by "natural" that which occurs without human intervention. But in this sense three-year-old children are "unnatural," since without human intervention in the form of care and support, a three-year-old would quickly perish.[27] And, in this sense, there is no such thing as "natural" bread, since, however free of additives and preservatives, bread has to be baked by people.

Still, we all understand that something constructed by humans, such as a parking lot, is quite different from a "natural setting" such as a wildlife refuge. What, then, is "nature"?

It is helpful to realize that while baking bread does not seriously interfere with the growth and development of other plants and animals, paving the ground with asphalt prevents grass and other plants from growing, deer from grazing, and so forth. This thought suggests a characterization of partnership with nature.

When human beings work with nature, the product of human ingenuity leaves room for other natural elements, such as trees, flowers, animals, ecosystems, and geological formations to realize their own special beauty and nature. A partnership with nature preserves the richness of the natural world. We must leave some wilderness unchanged by human effort, or we will forever lose a special and lovely feature of our world. We cannot and should not leave the whole world as wilderness. But when designing a structure to be built on a site with interesting natural features, such as old trees, a waterfall, or an interestingly shaped hill, the design should work with and preserve those features. Frank Lloyd Wright's ''Fallingwater'' is perhaps the most famous example. But working with a landscape need not be that expensive, nor does it require the genius of a Frank Lloyd Wright. A shopping center may ''fit into'' a hill, using the slopes as a design element. It may incorporate, or build around rather than raze, an old tree in the middle of the property, thus preserving a natural element and providing a pleasant environment for the shopper.

Partnership with nature means several things. First, we should make sure that we retain the special qualities of the natural world. We must not destroy all wilderness. We must not eradicate a species or destroy unique objects such as the Grand Canyon or the sequoia forests. In short, we must preserve the diversity and wonder of the natural world. Second, when we build or remake the world, we should be sensitive to the beauty of nature. For example, bridge design should work with the site, not against it. It is perverse to bulldoze the area around a highway in construction and then replant shrubs. The highways on which people most enjoy driving are those that interact with their natural setting. Highways should convey a sense of place. They should not be anonymous pipelines for shipping human cargo. Finally, our remaking of the world should be no more intrusive than necessary. Examples include preserving the flora when installing oil wells instead of clear-cutting the area to make access to and installation of the wells easier, building bird roosts over power lines, and using netting or sonic devices to keep sea life from becoming enmeshed in or killed by offshore facilities. (Every day ships throw 450,000 plastic containers in the sea. Five species of sea turtles confuse floating plastic bags and wraps for jellyfish [their food] and die. It is easy enough not to dump plastic garbage in the sea.)

While the idea of a partnership with nature is a powerful guiding idea, people cannot consider it a neat rule that will settle all disputes. We need two key elements to make it work. First, we must develop legal remedies and guidelines. These will necessarily be somewhat ad hoc, but the guiding judicial ideal should be that of a partnership with nature. Legal remedies must be used carefully, since they sometimes have unexpected results. For example, as a consequence of the Endangered Species Act, alligators are protected and no longer have commercial value. Unfortunately, instead of protecting alligators, this fact has led landowners to drain alligator habitats for farming.[28] Second, engineers must show sensitivity in their decisions and approaches to the demands of partnership with nature, so that legal problems are less likely to arise. Toward this end, engineers should cultivate an appreciation of nature in all its splendor and diversity. Go camping or hiking, develop an enjoyment and appreciation of flowers and animals, wetlands and forests, the early morning mist fluttering between the sentinels of dark cypress.

In sum, what characterizes the compleat engineer is not merely a commitment to particular gestures of this sort but a frame of mind. The compleat engineer feels a sense of kinship with and appreciation of the complex and multifarious beauties of the world about her, from the dainty lilt of the smallest wildflower to the majesty of the Alps. She enjoys camping or hiking or canoeing in the bayous, or sitting by the side of a pebbly brook. She views the earth and its other creatures as a partner and is as considerate and protective of them as she would be of a friend. Friends are not revered from afar, nor are they kicked about heedlessly. Rather, they are interacted with in a loving, caring, and mutually beneficial way. Indeed, some of the greatest feats of engineering have their roots in a love of nature. (For example, early aviationists learned much from their love of and study of birds.)

At the company level, partnership with nature means an increased concern with the environment. Monsanto Chairman Richard J. Mahoney, speaking at a National Wildlife Federation dinner, pointed out that "corporations like ours are experiencing what can only be called a revolution in environmental stewardship."[29] It is important to remember that a partnership should be mutually beneficial. Thus, engineers should look for ways to make taking care of the environment profitable. As George Pilko points out, "If a company can justify a wellness program because it reduces absenteeism and improves productivity, it can justify environmental expenditures on the same grounds. It not only is the moral and ethical thing to do, it makes sense on a dollars-and-cents basis."[30]

Environmental Considerations

While engineers should go the extra mile in planning for and avoiding hazards, accidents, and environmental harm, a certain amount of risk and environmental loss is inevitable. No activity is without risk, and so engineers should not be expected to eliminate every risk completely. Similarly, change is the only constant in life, and every change for the better leaves the world different from the way it was before. Some degree of environmental impact is inevitable. Every benefit has its price: in taking a step forward, one always loses something. Engineers and environmentalists must realize that nothing in life is all good and that even the most benign and beneficial decisions have their down side. This means that engineers should not be afraid to acknowledge any adverse effects of their projects, and environmentalists must accept some undesirable consequences as the price of a worthwhile project.

Thus, for any project, the risk and harm to the environment must be weighed against the benefit of the product or process and the cost of correcting the problem. This can only be accomplished rationally in the light of honest and unbiased information, combined with flexible and fair judgment. Unfortunately, companies sometimes overlook the indirect effects of their projects, and environmentalists often overlook the indirect costs of correcting a problem. Thus, it is useful to have some guidance in assessing environmental harm and in assessing the costs of correcting a problem.

The costs of correcting a problem involve both "resource costs" (that is, the money, labor, and so forth used to rectify the problem) and "factor income costs," the changes in capital income that result from rectifying the problem. The labor and cost of producing and installing smokestack scrubbers is an example of a resource cost. By contrast, if many companies switch from sulfurous coal to a less polluting fuel, the lower price of sulfurous coal becomes a factor income cost to coal-mining companies.[31]

For example, suppose company XYZ withdraws from the market a profitable, long-lived pesticide, in favor of a short-lived pesticide with fewer environmental consequences. XYZ suffers resource costs in developing, testing, marketing, and manufacturing the new pesticide and factor income costs to the extent that the profit earned on the new pesticide is less than that earned on the old pesticide. In addition, the new pesticide increases costs to farmers who use the pesticide, including resource costs such as the cost of buying the more expensive pesticide, the cost of more frequent applications, and the cost of any new equipment necessary to apply the new pesticide, as well as the factor income cost of decreased yield if the new pesticide is less effective in controlling pests.

In assessing the environmental effects of a project, one must consider the consequences, direct and indirect, of developing, manufacturing, using, and disposing of the product. A company that produces chemical fertilizer must factor in the effects on the environment that result from use of the fertilizer; the effects of mining, drilling for, or manufacturing materials used in producing the fertilizer; and the effects of depleting scarce resources used in producing the fertilizer. A firm that builds a dam designed to generate electricity must consider the environmental consequences of the dam's construction, such as cutting pathways to the dam for delivery of construction materials, the consequences for the river's ecosystem (such as the difficulty salmon may have in returning upstream), and the effects of the use of the electricity produced. Companies must also consider the costs of dealing with risks or environmental harms. These costs include the costs of safety drills, the costs of planning for and putting in place procedures for accidents, the costs of recalls that may be necessary, and the costs of lawsuits.

Environmental problems have at least three different kinds of solutions:

1. technical modifications of a process (e.g., adding scrubbers to smokestacks of coal-burning plants)
2. alternate technologies (e.g., using geothermal power instead of burning oil or coal)
3. nontechnological solutions

Engineers should ask several questions about the first two types of solutions, alternate technologies and technical modifications, including

Will it solve the problem with reasonable certainty?
Will the solution cause new problems, either technically, economically, or socially?

Could we, instead, substitute another technology that does not
cause this problem?
Could we do without the technology that causes the problem? Or
could we do with less of it?[32]

Questions that engineers should ask about nontechnological solutions include

Does this represent a real solution, that is, will it work, and is it
politically acceptable?
Is the idea economically justifiable, in that the cost is reasonable
compared to the benefits gained?
Is the idea socially justifiable? Who gains and who loses?[33]

For example, engineers should strive, when feasible, to
avoid thermosets, which are hard to recycle. Is the strength
and flexibility of thermosets really needed for this application? Are recyclable alternatives available that will work
adequately?

Similarly, chlorofluorocarbons (CFCs), which deplete
the protective ozone layer, take twenty to fifty years to
reach the ozone layer, as mentioned earlier. Thus, CFCs
released into the atmosphere today will continue to constitute a risk for our grandchildren. CFC-12 could be replaced
in cooling systems with a hydrofluorocarbon, HFC-134a,
but the latter costs more and may need replacement more
often. CFC-11 can be replaced in polystyrene with HCFC-
22, which does not insulate as well. Bioact (EC-7) is better
than CFC-113 for cleaning circuit boards, but it requires
new equipment and procedures.[34]

Given the complexity of these factors, it follows that
weighing the benefits of a project against its risk or
environmental impact is not easy. However, since engi-

neering is devoted to innovation in advancing human welfare in partnership with nature, engineers have a duty to use their abilities to discover ways to minimize the risks and environmental harms of their projects.

Of course, any company or firm has a limited expertise and budget. Engineers need not solve every problem their products may cause. So there are limits on what a company should be 'expected to do by way of protecting the environment. But an ethical firm is committed, to the extent feasible, to take reasonable steps to develop, promote, and encourage solutions to these problems.

This means that the ethical engineer's job is not finished when the product is perfected. He must also ask himself about the environmental effects of the product or process. The two principles of institutional accountability (see Chapter 4) suggest that he should take responsibility for doing what is feasible either to devise methods of minimizing harmful effects himself or to encourage the company to devise such methods or persuade others to do so. It is not his responsibility alone, but he must be a voice for good. This may take several forms, including (1) speaking to supervisors about the need to address the problem, (2) rewarding subordinates who work on or raise awareness of the problem, (3) speaking to legislators about the need to address the problem, or (4) publication of the problem in an appropriate forum (perhaps a trade publication or even a letter to the editor). Obviously, an employee contemplating one of the last two approaches should first consult his supervisors and should approach legislators or the public in a way that will not hurt the company. (It is generally possible to present the company as concerned and seeking solutions to this problem, rather than as an environmental villain.)

Illustrating Cases

Case 8: The company's product, Toxinal, is toxic to natural ecosystems or interferes with natural ecosystems in other ways (for example, nitrogen runoff from the use of Toxinal stimulates the growth of algae in rivers).

Discussion: The ethical engineer may choose from at least four responses to this problem:

1. When feasible, seek an alternative product or process that is not harmful or is less harmful than Toxinal. If this is not feasible, then investigate a different response.
2. Develop and publicize an additional product, process, or method of use that minimizes the harmful effects of Toxinal. (For example, when chemical fertilizers are applied to fields where seed has been poked into last year's stubble, rather than to fields that are burned and clear-cut, runoff is minimized.)
3. Publicize the problem and encourage solutions. Encouragement of solutions may take several forms, including providing research funding for a university to address the problem, lobbying state or federal agencies to fund research, or simply offering to assist and provide information to anyone working on a solution.
4. If the harm caused by Toxinal, even with the measures mentioned above, is serious enough, the company should consider taking Toxinal off the market.

Three questions are helpful in deciding whether to remove the product. First, how bad is the problem? Here the safety factors discussed above come into play. A rough guide to the extent of the problem can be obtained by subtracting the good done by the product, its manufacture, and its use (both directly and indirectly) from the harm done by the product, its manufacture, and its use (both directly and indirectly). However, as we saw earlier, this kind of purely quantitative analysis is inadequate. For example, severe harm to a few individuals matters more than minor inconvenience to a large number of people. And it makes a difference whether the risk or harm is limited to people who use the product voluntarily, knowing the risk.

Second, how much would the company suffer by removing the product from the market? Here, too, many factors come into play. How much of the company's revenue depends upon this product? How much overhead is tied up in the product? (This includes advertising, production machinery, inventory, etc.) How much of that overhead could be reutilized for another purpose (for example, how much would it cost to convert the Toxinal plant)? How difficult would it be for the company to replace this source of revenue? Does the company have sufficient capital resources to weather the changeover period? How many jobs would be lost?

Third, would removal do any good? (That is, what is the likelihood that were Toxinal removed, it would simply be replaced by another, equally harmful product?) This factor should not be used as an all-purpose excuse for unethical conduct. A hired killer cannot excuse his killings by saying that if he did not take the job, someone else would. If the harm done by Toxinal is bad enough, no ethical company would market it. However, the likelihood that someone else would market Toxinal (or an equally harmful product) is a mitigating factor. If the decision to remove Toxinal is a close one, this factor may make the difference.

Case 9: The process of making a specific product generates harmful effects. For example, cadmium is used in the manufacture of paints, alloys, light bulbs, pesticides, and nuclear reactor parts. Cadmium in the environment is accumulated by human food sources, including shellfish, rice, wheat, and fish liver. Once introduced into the body, cadmium accumulates in the kidneys and is associated with kidney disease and high blood pressure. Cadmium stays in the body a long time: it has a half-life of ten to thirty years. Many other chemicals commonly used in manufacturing contribute to health problems. For example, nitrates, which are added to meat for curing and are often found in fertilizer runoff, change hemoglobin from Fe^{++} to Fe^{+++}, which cannot oxygenate. Thus, nitrates cause slow suffocation, particularly in infants. Another group of chemical compounds, nitrosamines, have been found to be carcinogenic. The metallic element mercury—used as a preservative in latex paint and also used in paper mills, fungicides, electrical devices, and drugs—is a permanent pollutant that is recycled within the environment. Bacteria can change inorganic mercury, which is easily excreted, to more toxic alkyl mercury compounds, such as methyl mercury. Mercury is a nerve poison: the expression "mad as a hatter" originally described the effects of exposure to mercury on workers in the felt-hatting industry.[35]

Discussion: Here again, several responses are available. Generally speaking, we can modify the process to minimize the effects, institute ameliorating mechanisms (e.g., scrubbing pollutants from smokestacks, precooling water or pipes that may raise the temperature of rivers, etc.), or publicize the problem and encourage solutions.

Case 10: Accidents during the transportation or synthesis of a product may cause harm.

Discussion: Responses to this problem include designing transportation or synthesis processes to minimize risk, such as by including safety mechanisms and choosing the safest routes or sites, preparing (in advance) cleanup procedures and making sure cleanup can be rapidly and effectively instituted, instituting periodic safety drills and making sure that employees take these drills seriously, inspecting all of the above frequently, and publicizing the problem and encouraging solutions.

Case 11: Some safely manufactured products may do no harm while in use but nonetheless pose environmental problems after their usefulness has expired. Obviously, toxic materials such as nuclear waste pose a problem. But so do long-lived plastics. The long-term effects of turning the earth's resources into garbage are serious and cumulative. The ethical engineer must take responsibility for ensuring that neither the depletion of limited resources nor the production of garbage gets out of hand.

Discussion: When feasible, build biodegradability into the product. In any case, develop and publicize processes for reusing, or at least safely disposing of, the product.

While figures on recycling vary,[36] it is clear that much more can be done. For example, in the United States alone we discard 200 million tires each year. Although engineers have not yet been able to make pyrolysis (recovering oil from tires) work outside of laboratories, Tirecycle has combined the old tires with new rubber and various plastics to produce gaskets, storage bins, and railroad crossing pads. Similarly, 25 billion polystyrene containers are made each year in the United States. The National Polystyrene Recycling Company (formed by Dow, Amoco, Mobil, Atlantic Richfield, and others) grinds polystyrene into small pieces, washes it with hot water, fires it, and melts it at high temperatures, after which it is filtered, cooled, and chopped into pellets for reuse.[37] Although food containers cannot generally be purified enough for reuse with food, polyethylene terephthalate (PET), used in soda bottles, can be made into carpet fibers and backing, cushion stuffing, scouring pads, fiberfill, refrigerator insulation, and paintbrushes. Similarly, high-density polyethylene (HDPE), used in milk jugs, can be turned into construction materials (such as posts and boards), trash cans, and bins.[38]

Waste disposal also calls for engineering ingenuity. Among the techniques available for waste disposal are

1. neutralization (for example, lime applied to liquids from electroplating and steel finishing balances the pH and precipitates out heavy metal ions)[39]
2. oxidation and reduction (for example, cyanides are oxidized with sodium hydroxide and chlorine or sodium hypochloride)
3. ion exchange chromatography (unfortunately, still very expensive)
4. absorption on activated carbon
5. biological treatment (such as soil incorporation or land farming, which has been used with sludge from paper mills and fruit canneries, sewage sludge, pharmaceutical wastes, and petroleum refinery wastes)[40]
6. reuse or recycling (for example, the Timsfors Pulp Mill in Sweden flocculates fibrous wastewater with alums and reuses the resulting sludge in making low-grade paper;[41] the slurry in wet scrubbers can be used to produce gypsum, or the calcium or magnesium compound in the slurry may be recycled, thus producing sulfur or sulfuric acid for sale;[42] Amoco,

Rubbermaid, and McDonald's started a demonstration project in Brooklyn that sorted and recycled trash from school cafeterias and McDonald's restaurants)[43]

7. lagoon systems that remove biodegradable organics (BODs) but not nitrogen and phosphorus (these systems do not work well in winter)[44]

8. activated sludge processes (in which wastes are run through sludge)

9. reverse osmosis to concentrate solid wastes and recover water

These techniques can, of course be combined. For example, nitric acid wastes, used in etching silicon wafers, can be neutralized with lime. The resulting calcium nitrate can then be reused in fertilizer.[45] Moreover, one waste product can sometimes be used to neutralize another. For example, cyanide wastes can be used to reduce chromium VI wastes.[46] Moreover, waste solvents for electronics are sometimes of higher quality than the new materials used in other processes that tolerate higher levels of impurity. Thus, companies should make use of waste exchanges, which list available materials without identifying the source and then handle the exchanges.[47]

Case 12: The product or process of manufacture uses scarce, effectively nonrenewable resources.

Discussion: The following responses could prove useful. Minimize use of the scarce resource by finding an alternative or using as little as possible of the resource. Develop a method of extracting and reusing the scarce material. Develop a new method of extracting or a new source of the material. Publicize the problem and encourage solutions.

Case 13: You have an idea for an economical cooling method that would solve a major problem for your company. Unfortunately, the method involves heat exchange that would significantly raise the temperature of a river beyond the level tolerable to an endangered species of fish. How do you handle the problem? Should you present your idea for consideration? If you do, does your responsibility end at that point, or should you do more?

4

Additional Ethical Sources

Some ethical decisions are difficult and gut-wrenching. Others slip by unnoticed; an engineer may not realize, until it is too late, that something she has done is unethical. To make difficult decisions and avoid overlooking ethical problems, you need a large set of rules, principles, values, and guiding ideas. The more you have, the better decisions you will make. You are less likely to overlook an ethical problem if you ask yourself, before taking any important step, "Does this violate the duty to leave the world no worse? Does it treat others fairly and well? Does it respect rights? Does it violate the principle of universality? Am I promoting good consequences and showing respect for persons? Must I fight this battle?" You are better able to balance competing moral demands (such as a conflict between honesty and loyalty to your company) if you ask yourself "Are any institutional duties involved? What do the principles of accountability require of me? Should I break the rules in this case? How do the Golden Rule and the value of autonomy apply?" This chapter arms you with fifteen additional ethical sources you can use in making sound ethical decisions.

When to Fight a Battle

Morality is everyone's concern, and the engineer has a real stake in ensuring that his colleagues and company act ethically. The principles of accountability, the importance of a community atmosphere, and the ethical engineer's commitment to values such as fairness and safety together mean that no engineer can think unethical behavior in the workplace is "not my business."

Nevertheless, no one person can fight all of the world's ethical battles. For example, the ethical person is concerned about combating poverty and hunger; about improving education; about assisting in research and treatment for AIDS, cancer, lung disease, heart disease, and birth defects; about providing basic legal and medical care for all; about the problems of the handicapped and victims of discrimination and political repression, and so on. None of these problems is "not my business." However, no individual can contribute time or even money to all of these causes. Rather, the ethical person chooses to make a contribution to some of these causes, leaving the others for her fellow citizens. In the same way, the individual engineer must leave some moral battles to others.

One has no easy way to decide which moral battles one should fight, yet we must make this decision every time we encounter wrongdoing. Some factors help determine which moral battles one should fight: some moral battles must be fought, while some may be optional.

One may be required to fight a battle

1. as a matter of principle: the evil is so heinous that to remain silent is to ignore one's deepest moral commitments
2. as a matter of responsibility: one is directly responsible for righting the wrong
3. as a practical matter: the harm to oneself or one's goals is much greater than the harm one will incur by fighting
4. when there is no neutral option

Example 1: You have documented evidence that your company lied to a Senate subcommittee, suppressing facts proving that a current project has major design flaws and is being built with substandard materials, thus seriously threatening thousands of lives. This is a battle you must fight, because the evil involved is so great that you cannot in good conscience permit it to go unchallenged. You must, at the very least, speak to your supervisor about your concerns. (See also "Whistleblowing" in Chapter 5.)

Example 2: You are in charge of safety tests for a project, and the project supervisor orders one of your subordinates to falsify test results. This is a battle you must fight, because you are directly responsible for overseeing the integrity of the tests.

Example 3: In violation of regulations issued by the Occupational Safety and Health Administration, the plant in which you work registers dangerous levels of polychlorinated biphenyls (PCBs). This is a battle you must fight, because the PCB level poses a severe danger to you.

Example 4: You are subpoenaed as a witness by a court and are asked a question, the answer to which may harm your company. This is a battle you must fight, because you have no way to avoid the problem. When asked a compe-

tent question as a witness in a court of law, you have no
choice but to tell the truth, commit perjury, or be guilty of
contempt of court. It is impossible to "stay out of it."

Many of the morally troubling situations engineers face
are not like this; rather, the ethical engineer has some
choice about which moral battles to fight. There is a set of
battles, in other words, such that one must fight some, but
need not fight any given one. Although no formula exists
for deciding which of them to fight, certain considerations
make some decisions reasonable and others not.

When deciding which of these battles to fight, ask
yourself three crucial questions. First, how bad is the
infraction? In other words, what are the expected consequences to the persons who are hurt by the infraction? (It is
more important to fight to save a life than to avoid the
imposition of an unfair fifty-cent fine.) What is the moral
character of the infraction? (For example, suppose the dean
of the School of Engineering tells faculty who deserve to be
tenured, "Pay me ten dollars or I will see you don't get
tenure." Here the actual consequence is that the faculty
member has to pay ten dollars—not very significant. But it
is morally heinous that the dean uses her power this way.)
Second, what is the expected cost to me (and to other
nonguilty parties)? If the infraction is not severe, either
morally or consequentially, but the cost to me of fighting
would be disastrous, that is a good reason for choosing not
to fight this battle. Third, to what extent am I implicated? I
am more responsible for an infraction if I am in a special
position to know about or correct it, if I have close ties to
the infracting organization (for example, I am more responsible for what my department does than for what the

advertising department of another company does), if I played a role in the infraction itself (for example, I have to make out the pink slip), or if, in overlooking the infraction, I compromise doing my job faithfully.

Treating Others Fairly and Well

Several key elements contribute to the ethical engineer's ability to treat others in the work environment well and fairly.

First, fairness in the workplace requires people to be straightforward with each other. You should be direct and honest about a problem, even if that causes some tension. The straightforward approach often resolves problems or misunderstandings that would have remained unresolved had you been less direct. Give yourselves a chance to work things out. In any case, being straightforward with someone shows respect for him as a person. (Remember the point of the Golden Rule: would you prefer to be manipulated or to be treated straightforwardly?) Straightforwardness may cause some discomfort to you or to the other person, but when you deal with each other honestly both of you are acting as responsible adults, facing the situation squarely and honorably.

Second, you should be impartial. Always give other people a chance to present their side of things. This is important not only because it shows basic respect for others, but also because no matter how clear things seem to you, you may not have all the facts. Suppose you see Smith running out the door of Juarez's house, carrying a television. Juarez yells ''Stop,'' but Smith continues running.

Juarez tells you that Smith has just stolen his television. While the evidence seems convincing, Smith can prove her innocence simply by holding up a slip of paper, namely, the bill of sale for the television, marked "paid" and signed by Juarez. Perhaps Smith continued to run because she was in a rush. Perhaps Juarez lied to you because he did not want you to befriend Smith. Unless you speak to Smith, you cannot be sure that you have seen the whole picture. Refrain from jumping to conclusions. Moreover, avoid letting your personal feelings for or against someone cloud your judgment. Instead, judge on the basis of facts and sound evidence, not superficial appearances. Observe the principle of just deserts: people should be given what they deserve, and the way you treat people must be based on a fair assessment of the merits of each case, that is, of the relevant features.

Third, avoid exploiting or manipulating others. You do, of course, want to motivate and get good work out of your subordinates. Several things distinguish manipulation and exploitation from honest persuasion and motivation. One is deceit: you want to motivate your subordinates by being honest and straightforward. Another is taking advantage: do not make demands to which no reasonable person would agree if he had any choice at all. While it is hard to give a strict definition of exploitation and manipulation, it is usually fairly easy to tell when you are exploiting someone or being manipulative. In general, you want your relationships with subordinates to be mutually beneficial.

Fourth, help each person to make the most of herself. This effort is not only the ethical thing to do, but is good leadership as well. You want your department to be a good team in which everyone participates according to her unique talents and abilities. Development of a team requires that everyone have a stake in what is going on, that everyone's ideas are taken seriously, that people are treated as valuable individuals (not as replaceable and uniform machines), and that everyone has a chance to grow toward becoming the best she can be. To help each person to make the most of herself, you need to do five things: (1) allow scope for individual differences, (2) maximize opportunity for growth and taking responsibility, (3) encourage feedback and thoughtful participation, (4) reward and encourage effort, achievement, and commitment, and (5) be patient but firm.

Finally, you want to build a community atmosphere in your workplace, and you want to respect the rights of others, such as the right to privacy. Chapter 7, "Employer-Employee Relations," develops many of these ideas further.

Illustrating Cases

Case 14: Thorp, a reliable employee for several years, has been late rather frequently in the last month.

Discussion: The principles of being straightforward, not jumping to conclusions, and giving people a chance to present their side require that you speak to Thorp about this before coming to any conclusions. The goal of building a community atmosphere means that the conversation should be supportive rather than threatening—point out the lateness to Thorp and ask him if he has a problem with which you might be able to help. Invite Thorp to discuss the matter with you, not defensively, but as to a colleague on a team.

Now suppose, as a result of your discussion, you find that Thorp has been oversleeping because he has had to stay up with his ailing mother every night. Allowing scope for individual differences means that if some adjustment is feasible, it should be suggested. Perhaps Thorp could come in and leave an hour later while his mother is ill. This may not be practical: if Thorp's work requires him to interact with other engineers, it does no good to have him stay an hour after everyone else has left. If being an hour late now and then for a month or two does not pose a significant problem for the company, Thorp's lateness might be overlooked, provided it is clear that this situation is temporary. However, if Thorp's group is working feverishly to meet a contractual deadline, his lateness may mean losing the contract. So although you should try to make some adjustment, it may be impossible to do so. If you cannot accommodate him, and if Thorp's lateness does cause problems, then the problems caused by his lateness should be made clear to him, in a sympathetic rather than a hostile way.

The goal of building a community atmosphere suggests that personal and corporate gestures of concern for Thorp's mother are appropriate. Finally, being firm but patient suggests that, given the circumstances, you should expect Thorp to make a serious effort and cut down significantly the number of days in which he shows up late, but you should also realize that he may need some time to adjust: expect a serious effort from Thorp rather than perfection. If in the week following your discussion Thorp is late one day rather than three or four, tell him you are pleased at the progress he is making and that you have confidence that next week he will not be late at all.

Case 15: A subordinate of yours, Cleaver, has a good job at which she does well, but she will have no opportunity to advance at your firm, at least for some time. You become aware that firm Y is seeking someone with Cleaver's credentials for a more responsible position than your firm can offer her. Should you inform Cleaver of this opportunity? Does it matter if your awareness of the opportunity at Y resulted from your position (for example, a human resources officer at Y writes a letter to "Head of N Department" describing the opportunity and asking for a recommendation)?

Discussion: The goals of building a community atmosphere and maximizing opportunity for growth suggest you ought to feel some concern that Cleaver cannot advance and grow properly within your company. These factors suggest that you should inform Cleaver of the opportunity but at the same time tell her that you are happy with her work and hope she will stay. If the information comes to you as a result of your position, the case for informing Cleaver becomes even stronger: the principles of straightforwardness and not manipulating suggest that you should not use your position to keep such information from an employee. However, all these considerations must be balanced against your commitment to excellence and the company. How much of an opportunity is this for Cleaver? How hard will it be to replace her, and how much of a problem would her leaving cause? Is Y a competitor? (No company should be expected to undermine itself by going out of its way to provide its competition with top people.)

Some employers will ask, "Why should I go out of my way to lose a valuable employee?" The answer is that the long-term benefits of a community atmosphere are worth occasional minor sacrifices. No employer wants its employees to be willing to leave in the middle of an important project if a better-paying job opens with another company. Every employer wants its employees to be willing to put in extra hours when needed and to go the extra mile for the company. But an employer cannot expect employees to put loyalty to the company ahead of short-term personal advantage unless the company shows the same loyalty to employees. A company that expects loyalty from employees but will not make small sacrifices for the sake of its employees violates the principle of universality (discussed below). It is also kidding itself.

Case 16: You must decide whether to promote Perez or Johnson. Perez would do the job slightly better, but Johnson is more ''your kind of person.''

Discussion: Promoting someone because you like him violates the principle of just deserts: he has not earned the promotion, since your liking him is not a relevant reason for promotion. Nevertheless, Johnson's personal characteristics could be a job-related factor. If you think Johnson would be more supportive of his subordinates or could get more out of them, then you have relevant reasons for promoting Johnson over Perez.

The Duty to Leave the World No Worse

Professionals are also persons. Whatever is required of a professional by law and by company policy, he or she also has personal moral responsibilities that may not be overlooked. One personal responsibility holds special importance in professional life: we are each personally responsible for doing our best to ensure that, whatever we do, we do not leave the world worse off because of our activities.

What we do affects others, for better or worse. It is a worthy goal to make the world better than we found it. But even if we fail to improve the world in some way, we have a duty not to make the world worse than it would have been without us.[1] Just as campers must leave the forest in the same condition they found it and not scatter their litter about, so we have a general duty not to "trash up" the world as we find it. Obvious as this obligation might seem, professionals often overlook or ignore it. The duty of a engineer or corporate officer, some think, is to maximize profits for the company and its shareholders and not to look out for the rest of the world. Attorneys sometimes think their only duty is to the welfare of their clients, and politicians sometimes think that any kind of immorality is fine as long as it benefits their constituency. I am suggesting that anyone who makes the world a significantly worse place to maximize profits for the shareholders, to benefit her nation's foreign policy, or to help out a client fails to uphold her responsibilities as a human being and so acts wrongly.

Why do we have such a duty? Why not "trash up" the world if you can profit from it? This question has two answers. First, and most important, the duty to leave the world no worse lies at the center of living well, of leading a good life. It is a key to being a happy and fulfilled human being; the only alternative to the trivial, isolated, and unhappy "consumer life" is the life of value, and leading a life committed to values means trying to leave the world no worse. You must accept the duty to leave the world no worse if you do not want to live a life that is trivial, isolated, and unhappy. Second, we as citizens have the same duties to society that a company executive has to the company's shareholders.

How do the shortcomings of the consumer life show that we have a duty to leave the world no worse? In "A Revealing Case" in Chapter 1, we saw that because the consumer life is dedicated to the pursuit of feelings that are essentially private and fleeting, one who leads the consumer life is condemned to loneliness and frustration. People who have values, who care about justice and excellence for their own sake, have a stake in other people. And, since progress toward a value endures, someone with values can look back at his life and take satisfaction in what he has achieved. Unless I want to doom myself to the unhappiness and isolation of the consumer life, I must see myself as owing loyalty to values. If I value knowledge, then I think the world would be a better place without ignorance, and I commit myself to fighting ignorance. Either I am lonely and unhappy, or I am committed to making the world a better place. I should help when I can, of course, but at the very least I must not be a traitor to what I value, whether that be knowledge or excellence or human welfare. And so I have a personal responsibility to do my best not to make the world a worse place than I found it. In short, the only life worth living is the life committed to values, and you betray that commitment unless you do your best to leave the world no worse than you found it.

The second way of thinking about not "trashing" the world is more familiar. The shareholders of a corporation provide the capital for the corporation to operate, and so the executives of the corporation have a duty to serve the interests of the shareholders. In much the same way, society contributes the "opportunity capital" upon which we draw in everything we do. Without the efforts and struggles of those who lived before us, we would still be living in the stone age. No physician reinvents the history of medicine from her fertile brain; rather, she borrows her skills from the treasure trove of human knowledge, knowledge gained by generations of men and women who dedicated their lives to the battle against ignorance and disease. No modern business could operate without roads, water mains, sewer lines, currency, computers, telephones, and a large body of skills, techniques, and information, all of which are provided by society. No infant is born with engineering know-how or business sense and, whether formally or informally, must be taught to read and write and to understand the principles of business or engineering (perhaps by getting a degree at a university). Thus, every engineer, every executive, every physician, and every lawyer makes extensive use of society's educational system. In short, no one is "self-made." In an important sense, then, society is a stockholder in each of our lives, putting up the opportunity capital (of knowledge, services, etc.) we need to function in the modern world. Thus, we each owe society the loyalty that executives of a corporation owe its stockholders, and we have a duty to do our best not to put society in the red by our operations.[2] Thus, we have a duty to do our best not to make the world worse by our existence.

Given that we have this duty generally, how does it apply to engineering and business decisions?

Illustrating Cases and Examples

Case 17: In the 1970s, the Ford Motor Company had to decide whether to add to their Pinto model an improvement, costing $11 per vehicle, that would cause gas tanks to rupture less easily.[3] They did not do so. According to Mark Dowie in 1977, the Pinto was responsible for 500 to 900 "burn deaths to people who would not have been seriously injured if the car had not burst into flames."[4] Ford disputes these figures.

In any case, a report released by Ford's automotive safety director, J. S. Echold, entitled "Fatalities Associated with Crash-Induced Fuel Leakage and Fires" (Ford Motor Company, September 19, 1973), estimated that 180 burn deaths and 180 serious burn injuries could be prevented by making the $11 change. Multiplied by 12.5 million vehicles, this comes to a cost of $137 million. Since the report estimated the cost of each death at $200,000, each serious burn at $67,000, and each of the anticipated 21,000 burned vehicles at $700, for a total of $49.5 million, the report concluded that the $11 change was not cost-effective. (Ford eventually paid out $50 million in settlements and lost an untold amount in sales.)

Discussion: Considerable debate still rages about what a company owes its customers,[5] but clearly each purchaser derives minimal benefit through saving $11, while the pain and suffering of 360 deaths and serious injuries (using Ford's conservative figure) makes the world significantly worse. Those who decided not to make the $11 improvement violated their personal responsibility not to make the world worse and so acted wrongly.

The responsibility not to make the world worse also affects other Ford employees who were consulted about making the improvement. Everyone involved in the production of Pintos contributed to making the world worse. Those who knew about the problem but nevertheless worked on the Pinto violated their personal responsibility. Of course, each of us has many responsibilities that sometimes conflict. A plant worker also has responsibilities toward his or her family, and I am not insisting that workers with no say in the decision had a moral obligation to quit their jobs in protest. I am not even saying that every Ford employee who knew about the problem but did not speak out acted immorally, since we need not fight every moral battle. (See ''When to Fight a Battle'' earlier in this chapter.) But, since those who were aware of the problem had a personal responsibility not to engage in the making and selling of Pintos, each of them had to weigh this responsibility carefully against his other responsibilities, values, and duties. They each had a difficult moral choice to make.

Case 18: The Delta Company is considering closing or relocating its Smallville plant. The plant has been the major employer in Smallville for over fifteen years, and the economy of Smallville is thus highly dependent on the Delta plant. The plant is fairly profitable, though a marginally greater profit could be made by closing the plant and channeling operating funds to another plant. Is it ethical to close the plant?

Discussion: Some people think that closing the plant would violate the rights of the workers or that Delta owes it to the community to keep the plant open. However, much controversy and disagreement remains about what rights workers have and about what a company owes to the community.[6] Whatever the corporation owes or does not owe to workers and residents, another factor may not be overlooked. Decisions are made by people, and each of those people has a personal responsibility to make sure that the world is not worse off because of what she decides. You are clearly making the world worse if you change Smallville from a viable community into a depressed area, with all the hardship that involves for plant workers, area businesses, schoolteachers, and civic employees. All of this human pain and hardship is hardly offset by the effects of the small extra profit that Delta would make.[7] So if Delta decides to close the plant, those responsible for the decision have acted wrongly. In general, the duty to leave the world no worse means that corporations should not close reasonably profitable plants, should make every effort to make unprofitable plants profitable, and should seek to lessen the harsh effects of closing plants that must be closed.[8]

Example 5: Engineering and business decisions often affect the environment. Discussions of the effects of business operations on the environment tend to center on the "right [of citizens] to a liveable environment"[9] and on the economics of externalities and the social justice of apportioning negative effects. However these issues are decided, the individual engineer or executive has a duty to ensure that the operations he oversees do not make the world worse, and so he has a personal responsibility to mitigate or eliminate environmental harm caused by corporate operations. Just as in the Ford Pinto case (Case 17), this responsibility applies to everyone involved in the process that harms the environment, from the corporate executive officer to assembly-line workers.

Example 6: The television executive who fires an anchorperson because she is "too old" may or may not be violating her rights. But he is certainly making the world worse by supporting a system based on ageism or sexism, and he has a personal obligation, if not to take a stand against, at least not to help foster a system (of public perceptions and corporate behavior supporting those perceptions) that presents age as an unattractive liability. The same point applies to hiring decisions about receptionists, managers, and department heads.

Example 7: Sometimes it requires some thought to see that one's decisions leave the world worse off than it was before. P. V. Pumphrey, for example, points out that banking decisions can affect communities in six important ways: "[1] commercial loan policies can 'favor' certain industries, thus affecting competition and growth rates; [2] mortgage and home improvement loans can be made to or withheld from specific residential areas, thus affecting stability and values in the area; [3] new construction can be encouraged or discouraged by [the] availability of financing, with long-term impact on an area's tax base; [4] municipal financial stability can be encouraged or jeopardized by [a] bank's willingness or unwillingness to purchase notes and bonds; [5] personal loan policies can favor or exclude certain population groups, promoting or restricting social mobility; and [6] international loans can support oppressive foreign regimes; they can support the internal controls exercised over populations."[10] Similarly, television advertisements as a group heavily influence the values of our society. A series of advertisements for *Time,* showing families and friends discussing the news in a friendly and supportive way, exerts a positive influence, while advertisements that promote less healthy values exert negative influences. Each of us has a responsibility to examine the less obvious consequences of our work decisions.

One final case helps answer an important objection. Some people have argued that one's personal moral responsibilities stop when one enters the plant or office. They insist that the job of the executive or engineer is to make money for the company and that the job must take precedence over personal moral qualms. If the people urging this view are right, then you should ignore the duty to leave the world no worse when making business decisions. The next case illustrates the conflict between their view and what I am suggesting.

Case 19: Jones is the president of a tobacco company. Smith, a bright young member of the advertising department, suggests to Jones that the company could raise its current return of 10 percent to 12 percent by marketing He-Man cigarettes, which are unusually high in tar and nicotine. Although at present no one would purchase such a product, Smith's research shows that a demand for He-Man cigarettes could be created by an ad campaign that plays on buyers' fears about their masculinity, using slogans such as "Only wimps smoke low-tar cigarettes" and "Real men smoke He-Man cigarettes." Jones has no reason to think that if she does not authorize marketing the product, some other tobacco company will market a similar product. Jones must decide whether to authorize the product and ad campaign.

Discussion: This case clearly shows a conflict between maximizing profits and not making the world a worse place. If Jones does not authorize production, the company will probably earn less than it otherwise would. If Jones does authorize production, with the relevant advertising, she must admit, if she is honest, that she is deliberately setting out to induce others to do things that would make the world a place of greater misery and hardship.[11] Now, you might be tempted to say, "No one forces the buyer to purchase He-Man cigarettes. It is his health and his money, and he must be the one to make the decision whether to smoke He-Man cigarettes or not. It is the buyer, not the manufacturer, who must take the responsibility." This might be true: perhaps I do not owe it to you not to help you hurt yourself, and perhaps I do not even owe it to you not to try to induce you to hurt yourself.

But another issue emerges here. By marketing He-Man cigarettes, the businesswoman fails to meet one of her personal obligations as an individual, namely, her duty to try not to make the world a worse place. This is not a duty she owes to the particular consumer who would be hurt by smoking He-Man cigarettes. Rather, not trashing up the world is an entrance requirement to the moral community. If one wants to live anything more than the consumer life, one must take personal responsibility to see that one's life not be a blight. The executive who authorizes the marketing of He-Man cigarettes shirks this responsibility.

You may bear the responsibility for destroying your own life with heroin, and it may be, in some sense, your choice. But my commitment to what I value requires me not to assist you by providing the heroin and especially not to try to induce you to use heroin. The executive may not adopt the morality of the pimp and the drug pusher, washing her hands of the responsibility for providing others with what they want. Even if drug pushers and pimps do not violate the rights of the addict and the john, what they are doing is wrong. I do not use the metaphor of prostitution lightly. It is sometimes said that an executive, as an agent of the corporation's owners, has no right to substitute his own moral judgment for the corporation's explicit purpose, which is to make money.[12]

This argument is sound, however, only if it is morally permissible to offer and accept employment that requires violating moral duties. But there are real limits on what one may licitly accept money to do. After all, the hit-person and the prostitute cannot excuse their actions by declaring that they are just doing what they are paid to do. The executive or engineer who accepts an employment contract calling for him to violate his personal moral responsibilities becomes a kind of prostitute, doing immoral things for money. And the stockholders who insist on such a contract are using economic coercion to drive executives and engineers into a life of moral prostitution. In any case, it is a defensible principle of contract law that contracts calling for immorality are not enforceable since they are contrary to public policy, and it is a defensible principle of ethics that one ought not to keep a promise to do wrong. Thus, a contract asking engineers or executives to act immorally by violating their personal moral responsibilities as human beings has no standing.

Respect for Persons

The philosopher Immanuel Kant tells us that we should always treat people as ends, never merely as means. For example, when I put money in a candy machine, I am using the machine merely as a means of getting candy. If the machine jams, I might kick the machine: I do not worry about the machine's feelings. When I give fifty cents to a store clerk for a candy bar, I am also treating the clerk as a means of getting candy. But the clerk is not merely a means, that is, I do not kick the clerk if he is too slow in giving me my change. I resist kicking the clerk because I recognize that he is also a person who has feelings that count and a sense of personal worth and dignity that I must respect.

Respect for persons has two related aspects. First, you should not use people. "Avoid exploiting or manipulating others," one of the rules discussed in "Treating Others Fairly and Well," is only one application of the idea that one should not use people. Engineers will discover many other applications of this idea in their professional and personal lives.

It is unethical, for example, to let a subordinate think she will get a promotion if she completes a task well, when that is not the case. True, her misunderstanding does serve to motivate her, and in the short run you will increase productivity by not correcting her mistaken impression. But you are acting unethically in using her this way, and, in the long run, it is bad business practice. It is also unethical to pursue a social relationship with someone you dislike because that person can advance your career. When you do that, you are exploiting the person because your offer of friendship is a fraud. In some ways this is worse than lying about a termite problem to a prospective buyer of your house. In both cases you are obtaining something by fraud that you might not get if you were honest. In the termite case, you are taking advantage of another person as a buyer. When you pretend to feel friendship, you are taking advantage of another person as a person.

Second, you should treat others with dignity and respect. It is easy to make others feel small and to do little things that undermine their sense of dignity and worth. Although some things, necessarily, distinguish an executive from a secretary, try to avoid unnecessary distinctions that say to the secretary, ''You're just a secretary.'' While in some cases it may serve a useful purpose to have separate entrances for executives and subordinates, having separate entrances is often just a way of making subordinates feel that they do not count as much. On the positive side, one can communicate respect to a subordinate in many subtle ways. For example, saying ''Please do X'' or ''Could you do X?'' is better than giving an order.

Rights

One crucial rule that applies not only to engineering but to every facet of ethical conduct is ''Respect the rights of others.'' Our society was founded on the principle that people have rights. People are entitled to free speech, for example, and so we have to allow people to speak freely even if their speaking causes us much inconvenience or does much harm. Two basic kinds of rights exist: permission rights and entitlement rights. If society is obligated to provide everyone with a minimal education, that is an entitlement right: people are entitled to receive an education. The right to free speech, by contrast, is a permission right. It does not mean that everyone is entitled to free air time or newspaper space but that society may not restrict, interfere with, or prevent people from trying to get their views across. People must be given an education (entitlement) and must be left free to do what they can to get their views aired (permission).

In addition, there is a difference between legal rights and moral rights. Legal rights are the entitlements and permissions the law gives people. Legal rights change as the law changes. For example, suppose the Texas legislature passes a law requiring employers to give two weeks of paid vacation to all full-time employees. As a result, all full-time employees in Texas have a legal (entitlement) right to two weeks of paid vacation. This is a legal right that employees in Montana do not have. By contrast, moral rights are not a matter of law but of ethics and (generally) apply equally to everyone. Although infidelity is not a crime in most states, spouses in a traditional marriage have a moral right to expect their spouses to be faithful. (Of course, many moral rights are also legal rights, such as the right not to be murdered.) Engineers must be scrupulous about observing legal rights and should be sensitive to moral rights.

Two kinds of moral rights exist: special moral rights and basic moral rights. Special moral rights stem from particular relationships, such as marriage. My children have special moral rights on my time and loyalty that other children do not have. Basic moral rights concern the basic needs people have in order to participate as full citizens and moral beings in their society. Ignorant people cannot participate rationally in the public life of the community, so education is a basic moral right. People cannot participate in the public life of the community if they are not free to argue and express their views, so free speech is a basic moral right. (In our legal system, of course, free speech is also a legal right.) People cannot function as moral agents if they lack reasonable opportunities to become involved in shaping their own destinies, nor can they function as distinct individuals if they have no privacy.

It is important to notice that the right to free speech does not mean that you may say anything at all. Rather, it means that each person must be given adequate opportunity to debate, reason, voice his or her views, and so forth. Similarly, the right to education does not mean that you must be taught anything you wish to learn. The right to education is really two rights: an entitlement right that each person be given enough education to be able to function as a rational citizen, and a permission right that each person be given adequate opportunity for self-development.

An engineering company must operate in a way that respects these rights, so central to our way of life.

Illustrating Case

Case 20: Jackson is an engineer employed by Universal Chemical, a large company. Universal manufactures DN3, a chemical with several industrial uses. Were the Defense

Department to resume production of materials for chemical warfare, a significant amount of DN3 would be used in the manufacture of chemical weapons. Jackson writes a strong letter to a national magazine denouncing chemical warfare as immoral and urging citizens to tell their representatives to oppose a newly introduced bill authorizing the production of chemical weapons.

Discussion: In writing this letter, Jackson was properly exercising her constitutional right to advocate her moral views. Universal Chemical has a moral obligation not to cast a ''chilling effect'' on this right by penalizing Jackson in any way, direct or indirect, for writing the letter, even though the letter urges a course that would eliminate a financial benefit to the company. For example, Jackson's superiors must make an effort not to view the letter as evidence that Jackson lacks team spirit. Moreover, Jackson should not be given the impression that her letter will count against her.

Several factors are important here. Jackson's letter did not breach the duty of confidentiality by revealing trade secrets or sensitive company information. In addition, Jackson's letter did not attack the company or criticize its actions. Thus, writing the letter constituted neither disloyalty to the company nor avoiding proper channels. DN3 has other industrial uses, and Jackson did not suggest that DN3 be withdrawn or outlawed. (By contrast, if Jackson claimed that DN3 posed a danger to public safety and should not be produced, she would have a duty to address the problem within corporate channels before writing a letter to the magazine. See ''Whistleblowing'' in Chapter 5.)

Autonomy

Autonomy is always a value and, in some cases, may be a right as well. Autonomy is one of the most important values of a free society. No one likes to be bossed about and told what to do, but the value of autonomy extends deeper than this. A central premise of our way of life is that people should be responsible for themselves. People are moral agents and have a responsibility as well as a right to play a role in shaping their own futures. We are a community of people, not of ants. Ants have particular roles to play (gathering food, defending the colony, etc.), and they fulfill their roles without question. One worker ant is very much like another. By contrast, people have individual needs and abilities, and each person has his own ideas about what is good, about how one ought to live, and about what is important. Each person must participate in his own way in the common life of the community.

For engineering ethics, this individuality means that engineers must treat people as having special value (see ''Respect for Persons'' above) and respect other people's desire to make decisions for themselves. Treating people as having special value means that the ethical engineer does not treat people as a commodity, interchangeable and replaceable. The loss of a life should not be treated as just another dollar figure, as in the Pinto case. Respecting other people's desire to make decisions for themselves means that the ethical engineer does not treat adults like small children unable to make intelligent decisions about their own lives. This is why the discussion in Case 1 (in Chapter 1) advised you to avoid taking steps that might have a major impact on Jones' career without consulting her. Jones should have some say in what happens to her. This is why a community should have some say about the risks imposed on it by an engineering project, such as a nuclear power plant. This is why voluntary risks are preferable to involuntary risks.

Nevertheless, although autonomy is an important value, it is not an absolute value. Other things count, too. A company does not have to scrap its plans to build a plant because one resident dislikes it or thinks that the risk is not worth the benefit. Moreover, marketing a cancer-causing lipstick is not necessarily ethical just because buyers know the risk and are willing to take it. (See Case 2 in Chapter 3.) Life is full of compromises, and autonomy is one of the things that must sometimes be compromised. Autonomy must be weighed against other values. However, when Jones' autonomy is so severely compromised that she is denied a say in the most crucial and important decisions about her life, her rights have been violated, and it is almost never ethically acceptable to violate other people's rights. (See "Rights" above.)

To summarize, two points must be kept in mind. First, the ethical engineer should always try to respect autonomy, though autonomy must be balanced against other values and rules. So in deciding between different options, it counts against an option that the option violates someone's autonomy, though other factors may count more strongly in favor of the option. Second, if an option would severely violate someone's autonomy, this might violate a right, and so choosing the option would violate a specific rule to respect the rights of others.

Principles of Accountability

For what are we morally accountable? Put another way, what is my responsibility as an ethical engineer? After all, the engineer is only one person in a company, and the company only one institution within a society. The individual engineer cannot take responsibility for everything. He cannot even take responsibility for all the consequences of his own actions, since, very often, we cannot know or control all the consequences of what we do.

Frank Collins suggests that "there are three ways in which the special responsibility of engineers for the uses and effects of technology may be exercised. The first is as individuals in the daily practice of their work. The second is as a group through the technical societies. The third is to bring special competence to the public debate on the threatening problems arising from destructive uses of technology."[13]

Mike Martin and Roland Schinzinger suggest that "from the perspective of engineering as social experimentation, . . . the general features of morally responsible engineers [are] . . . a conscientious commitment to live by moral values, a comprehensive perspective, autonomy and accountability.[14] Or, stated in greater detail . . . 1) A primary obligation to protect the safety of and respect the right of consent of human subjects. 2) A constant awareness of the experimental nature of any project, imaginative forecasting of its possible side effects, and a reasonable effort to monitor them. 3) Autonomous, personal involvement in all steps of a project. 4) Accepting accountability for the results of a project."[15] Here "accountable" means not only "being culpable and blameworthy for misdeeds," but also "the general disposition of being willing to submit one's actions to moral scrutiny and be open and responsive to the assessments of others. It involves a willingness to present morally cogent reasons for one's conduct when called upon to do so in appropriate circumstances."[16] Unfortunately, it is not always easy to live by these strict standards of accountability.[17] The engineer has to balance her personal responsibility against her willingness to be part of a team.

A better approach to accountability is the principle of institutional responsibility. You have to put considerable trust in the larger institution of which you are a part. You cannot be a one-person watchdog committee. But your trust in the company should not be blind trust: you should keep an ear open, and you should not ignore signs of trouble. In short, you should be aware of the effects of your actions on the company as a whole, and you have some duty to keep an eye on how the company operates. We can summarize this ideal in two sentences. The first principle of institutional responsibility is that you are responsible for seeing to it that your participation in a project, in your company, in the profession, and in society generally supports and leads to an ethical outcome. The second principle of institutional responsibility is that you are responsible for monitoring, to the best of your (often limited) ability, the ethical character of your company, profession, and society, and taking whatever steps are warranted when that institution goes astray.

One application of the second principle (the duty to monitor the company's activities) merits special notice. Engineers must be alert for what David Frew calls "synergism."[18] Frew interviewed employees of a heavily polluting company, from the president down, and realized that "although each interviewee recognized his organization's role as a polluter, none either was acting in a way [that] would be interpreted . . . as [directly] causing the pollution, nor was any individual in a position to end or . . . significantly change the process."[19] The ethical engineer will look out for such effects, give some thought to what could be done to change them, and bring these observations to the attention of appropriate superiors.

If you are asked to treat an employee unfairly, falsify data, or perform other unethical actions, doing so would clearly violate the first principle of institutional accountability: your conduct would be aiding and abetting unethical corporate behavior. The second principle applies when your action or project, in itself, may not be clearly harmful. You may come to have knowledge or suspicions about other projects of the company or about the big picture of which your project is but a small part. Case 27 in Chapter 5 (based on the B.A.R.T. case) is an example. This second principle does not require you, single-handedly, to take responsibility for correcting the wrong. It requires rather that you ask yourself, "What feasible and warranted steps could I take?" The answer will depend on the particular case.

Institutional Duties

Rules sometimes conflict. When they do, engineers need to decide which rule has greater weight. One factor in weighing conflicting rules is that institutional duties have special importance.

Institutions such as engineering, journalism, and medicine have special duties. Because medicine is an institution devoted to health, physicians have a special duty to promote health: a physician has a special duty to stop and aid the victim of an auto accident when he drives past a wreck. Similarly, while the rule "Don't spread (unsupported) rumors" applies to everyone, it is much worse for a journalist to spread an unsupported rumor than it is for just anyone to do so. After all, journalism as an institution has a special commitment to accurate reporting, and so the journalist has a special obligation to report accurately.

Engineers also have special institutional duties, including the duties to protect public safety, to use technological know-how to further human welfare, to keep accurate records and perform adequate tests, and to work in partnership with nature. The rules that reflect these duties have special weight, and this gives them an edge when they conflict with other rules.

It is helpful to understand just what institutional duties are and why they are of special importance. By an "institution" I mean an important organization or clearly defined body that has a socially recognized role it is expected to perform and is governed by socially recognized rules, procedures, and practices. For example, in our society, the health care profession is an institution. Because the state licenses health care professionals, the health care profession has a clearly defined body of doctors, nurses, hospitals, nursing homes, and other providers of services. The health care profession has a clear, socially recognized role, namely, attending to health. The way that physicians and therapists attend to health is determined by certain well-understood roles, such as those of physician and nurse, and health care professionals are expected to follow socially recognized practices. (So faith healers and Aunt Tillie's habit of starving your cold and feeding your fever do not count in this definition.)

Engineering is also an institution. It is usually clear who is an engineer and who is not.[20] Engineering has a socially recognized role: safely advancing the progress of the human community, in partnership with nature, through know-how used in a systematic practice of clear, clean, practical decision making. And it performs its role through well-understood roles and practices.

Institutional duties are created when an institution cannot function without public trust in the institution's faithfully performing its task according to its practices and roles. For example, if the public could not trust audit accountants to use standard accounting procedures to provide an accurate and exact picture of a company's financial situation, there would be no reason to hire audit accountants. The institution of accounting, one might say, makes a kind of public promise to do this and functions as a profession only because people trust accountants to keep this promise. So accountants have an institutional duty to keep or create accurate records in accordance with standard accounting procedures.

In the same way, engineering as a profession depends upon public trust. If company X is known to do shoddy, inaccurate, or falsified tests, no rational society will allow X to build a bridge, a nuclear facility, or a chemical plant. Similarly, no manufacturer will purchase a synthetic plastic from X unless the specifications of that plastic are reliable.

In general, if people could not rely on the implicit promise of engineering as a profession to perform its social role faithfully, the profession of engineering could not function as it does.

Therefore, engineers have special institutional duties to protect public safety, to use technological know-how creatively to further human welfare, to work in partnership with nature, and so forth. An engineer who does not go out of her way to protect the safety of the public thus violates a special trust, a trust she invites by becoming an engineer.[21] Everyone, of course, has a moral duty not to endanger other people. Everyone also has a stake in advancing human welfare. But engineers have a special institutional duty to safety and human welfare that goes well beyond the general moral duties nonengineers have: by joining the institution of engineering, engineers become obligated to give greater weight to safety and welfare and to go further in their pursuit of safety and welfare than other people. Similarly, engineers have a special institutional duty to perform thorough and reliable tests and to keep accurate and precise records of those tests, to respect nature, and to obey legal requirements, in letter and in spirit.

These institutional duties put great pressure on the engineer not to falsify tests, even if that means losing one's job or harming the company. As always, there are exceptions: an engineer forced by the Nazis to develop efficient methods of exterminating Jews ought to sabotage that project if he can. But the exceptions are rare. Usually, because institutional duties have great weight, they must not be violated.

Models of the Professions

Moral conclusions about professional conduct can be drawn from the model one gives of a profession generally and of engineering in particular.

Definitions of a "profession" are plentiful.[22] Michael Bayles identifies three features necessary for an occupation to count as a profession: (1) extensive training, (2) a significant intellectual component, and (3) providing an important service in society.[23] Bayles also lists three common features of professions: (4) a process of certification or licensure, (5) an organization of members that promotes the goals of the profession and the economic well-being of its members, and (6) room for autonomy in one's work. To these six I would add a seventh feature: (7) the field constitutes an institution that functions because of public trust.

The purpose of a definition is to point out key features that have moral significance. What lessons can we draw from this definition?

First, extensive training, the intellectual component, providing a crucial service, licensure, and, to a lesser extent, organization of members (features 1, 2, 3, 4, and 5) together mean that professionals have a coercive bargaining position. In a free bargaining situation, people are free to make whatever agreement they wish. For example, I do not owe it to my neighbor to mow his lawn for him, so I may offer to mow his lawn in exchange for the deed to his house. This is an exorbitant demand, of course, but as he is quite free to turn down my offer, it is up to him to decide whether having his lawn mowed is worth giving up his house. By contrast, suppose he is drowning in a secluded lake and I am standing on the edge of the lake with a life preserver. It is unethical to refuse to throw him the life preserver unless he promises to give me his house, and no court would uphold such a ''contract.'' This is not a free bargaining position but a coercive bargaining position, and I am not legally or morally entitled to exploit him this way. (Similarly, contract law refuses to uphold ''contracts of adhesion.''[24]) Our definition of a profession reveals that professionals are generally in a coercive rather than a free bargaining position: the importance of the service and legal licensure mean that the professional has a monopoly on a service that society cannot really do without, and (because of the extensive training and intellectual component) society cannot easily replace the professional who ''strikes.''

Moreover, clients lack the organization that membership in professional societies provides. Thus, unrestricted rules of bargaining do not apply to the professional as they might to a gardener. So professionals are morally required to exercise restraint in what they demand in exchange for their services. One consequence of this conclusion is that physicians and attorneys are not morally justified in demanding the very high fees some of them require. Another is that engineers have a moral obligation to look out for the public interest, since those adversely affected by engineering projects are not always in a position to bargain effectively.

Second, extensive training, the intellectual component, providing an important service, and autonomy (features 1, 2, 3, and 6) indicate the need for professional self-regulation: because the service is important and quality is crucial (the public has a legitimate interest in the exercise of the profession), and because the professional is largely autonomous and evaluation of professional work requires difficult-to-obtain expertise, outside regulation is less feasible than it is in other areas. Thus, engineering as a profession has a special duty to regulate the competence and ethics of practicing engineers. For the individual engineer, this means participating in professional societies. It means taking some responsibility to see that incompetent or unethical colleagues do no harm. This may mean reporting them, not "covering up" for them, or simply speaking to them.

Third, the intellectual component, the importance of the service, and licensure (features 2, 3, and 4) indicate that professionals owe a debt of gratitude to society: the granting of a monopoly, the training that social institutions such as universities provide, and the social institutions of the professions themselves mean that professionals' skills are obtained and employed only by virtue of considerable assistance from their society. How this debt of gratitude should be repaid depends on the profession. In general, professionals have a special duty to be good public citizens and to use their skills for the public good.

Finally, the importance of the service and the necessity for public trust (features 3 and 7) together mean that professionals have a special responsibility toward society, which entrusted them with an important service.[25]

Another source of ethical insight is the way one views the engineering profession in particular. Martin and Schinzinger mention six possible models of the engineer: (1) a "savior" who will create utopia and rescue society from the ills of poverty, inefficiency, and so forth; (2) a "guardian" who can best guide society in its development; (3) a "bureaucratic servant" who simply "translates the directives of management into concrete achievements"; (4) a "social servant" who turns society's commands into concrete achievements; (5) a "social enabler and catalyst" who, while ceding ultimate authority to management or society, must help them to "understand their own needs and to make informed decisions about desirable ends . . . and means"; and (6) a "game player" who simply plays by the corporate rules to win and move ahead.[26]

Of these, model 5 is clearly the most acceptable. Model 1 is ruled out by the value of autonomy, models 3 and 4 are ruled out by the duty to leave the world no worse, and model 6 is ruled out by the value of community. Model 2 simply becomes model 5 when the importance of autonomy is fully appreciated. So model 5 seems the most appropriate. Two important things follow from this model.

First, engineers as a group have a duty to offer their professional perceptions about the needs of society and technological problems facing the community. Within the company, this means speaking up to supervisors and management about public policy, to the extent one knowledgeably can. In addition, engineers may have a special perspective on noncompany matters (such as national energy policy, what kind of publicly funded research is likely to prove useful, etc.). Engineers as a group have a duty to testify before legislative committees, write articles or give interviews to the press about technologically oriented public issues, and so forth. In short, engineers who, because of their expertise, have a special perspective on public issues should make their voices heard.

Second, the public must be involved in important engineering decisions that affect the life of the community. Companies can help achieve this result by establishing an environmental and community issues advisory board. (See Appendix 1.)

Promoting Good Consequences

One important question to ask when deciding whether to do something is "What will happen if I do that?"[27] In other words, we can do a cost-benefit analysis of the different options open to us. We must remember to consider all the costs and benefits, long-range as well as short-range, psychological and moral as well as physical, indirect as well as direct, and less obvious as well as more obvious. For example, while harsh penalties for nonperformance might improve productivity in the short run, such a policy may have detrimental indirect, long-term psychological consequences, such as souring the atmosphere and diminishing team spirit. Moreover, while sometimes we should look at the consequences of particular acts, sometimes we should look rather at the consequences of policies.[28] For example, while it might be easiest to transfer a particular employee without telling him in what respects his work is unsatisfactory, keeping hidden the reasons for such decisions would be a bad policy: the best policy is to be direct with employees, to let each employee know exactly where he stands. Knowing when to look at an act in isolation and when to think in terms of general policy is one of the hardest and most important things to learn in thinking ethically.

Several factors count toward thinking in terms of policy. There is reason to prefer enforcing a general policy when it is important for people to be able to form secure expectations about the sort of thing at issue, when treating each case individually would lead to unfairness, or when the matter in question is important to the institutional character of the professional or corporate setting. Other factors count toward thinking in terms of particular acts. There is reason to treat cases individually when cases substantially differ from one another or when the harm or unfairness in a particular case outweighs the benefits of a policy. These factors have to weighed when making particular decisions.

For example, the best approach to dealing with a struggling employee varies considerably from employee to employee, because people are very different. An approach that would be successful with one person would be disastrous with another. Thus, there is some reason to treat struggling employees on a case-by-case basis. Since, however, it is unlikely that transferring an employee without informing him of his shortcomings will make him a better engineer, this factor does not give us a strong reason for skirting the general policy of letting engineers know how they stand and in exactly what ways their work is unsatisfactory. Employees need to be able to have secure expectations about how dissatisfaction with their work will be handled, and secrecy about such matters undermines the community atmosphere of the corporation. (See ''When to Break the Rules'' later in this chapter for further guidance.) Thus, one should follow the policy and tell the struggling employee frankly in which respects his work is unsatisfactory.

Although promoting good consequences is an important aim of ethical decision making, it is not the only aim. Some things are wrong to do, however good the consequences, and some things one must do, however bad the consequences. The conflict between promoting good consequences and other moral factors is one of the major sources of ethical dilemmas. Two factors set limits on promoting good consequences: it is important to live in a moral environment, to be part of a moral community; and you should live in a way that proclaims your values and ideals.

Illustrating Example

Example 8: Jones and Smith are rival candidates for a promotion. Smith needs the promotion more and would be better in the job. Although the overall consequences of telling lies about Jones so Smith will get the job might be beneficial, it would be wrong to do this. Shafting one person to help another person even more is inconsistent with a moral environment and undermines the moral community. Being part of a moral community requires an environment of trust in which treating people unfairly, even to help someone else, is not tolerated. Moreover, if you tell lies about Jones, your conduct, however good its hidden motives, does not proclaim your commitment to honesty and fair dealing.

Universality

One important technique of ethical thought is to ask "What if everyone did that?"[29] Morality, after all, plays no favorites: no one can justifiably say, "None of you should lie, but I'm special, so I may lie whenever I feel like it." The principle of universality states that similar cases should be treated the same way, and so, generally, I should not do something if it is wrong for everyone else to do it. For example, suppose six farms are threatened by flooding unless a retaining wall is built. The sixth farmer refuses to help build the wall, knowing that the other five have no choice but to build the wall by themselves. Here the sixth farmer violates the principle of universality. If everyone refuses to do his share, calamity results. The sixth farmer recognizes the need for the wall and wants the other farmers to do their share. He intends to get a free ride: he can afford to shirk his responsibilities because others do their duty. Clearly, shirking one's duty in this way is unethical. It is wrong to take advantage of the fact that others (and not you) are doing the right thing. Thus, you should ask yourself, when evaluating an option, "What if everyone did that?"

Used wrongly, this technique leads to error. It would be disastrous for our society if everyone in it became a physician—no crops would be planted, no roads or houses would be built, no toasters or medicine would be produced, and no professional opera or sports would enliven leisure hours. This does not make it wrong to become a physician. Rather, what is involved is a question of fairness: do not be a parasite or a free rider. The cases and discussions below help clarify the proper use of the principle of universality.

Illustrating Examples

Example 9: Hiring away. Engineering firms have formed a kind of "gentleperson's agreement" not to raid other firms: although no laws or legally binding contractual duties forbid the practice, engineering firms have an implicit understanding that they will not "hire away" employees from each other. A human resources officer who violates this agreement, while relying on it to prevent other firms from inducing her own employees to leave, thus violates the principle of universality: she is freeloading, enjoying the benefits of the rule without doing her part to pay the price. She is, in effect, saying, "The rules apply only to other people, not to me. I'm special. You people must obey the rule and pay the price of not taking engineers away from other firms, but not me." Morality does not play favorites this way: no one is a morally privileged character. (See Case 49 in Chapter 7.)

Example 10: Lying. Lying involves more than saying something false. Suppose you go to a movie, and in the movie the lead actor says, "I'm from Idaho." This is not a lie, even if the actor knows quite well that he hails from Louisiana. He is merely performing his lines in the script. But if I say in a job interview that I am from Idaho, this is a lie. I am lying in this context because we usually have a social understanding that we will tell each other the truth: the social rules of job interviewing are based on a mutual understanding that both parties are supposed to tell the truth. When we go to a movie, however, we all understand that the actors in the film will be reading a script, not telling the truth about themselves. In other words, you can only lie in a situation governed by the social rule of telling the truth. Otherwise, like the actor's statement that he is from Idaho, what you say will have no tendency to deceive.

Thus, lying is abusing a social rule, trying to deceive someone by taking advantage of the social rule that we are supposed to tell the truth. You can lie to someone about where you were last night only because we have a social rule that such questions are to be answered truthfully. We could not function as a society without this rule (imagine what it would be like if any question you asked of a fellow worker, a physician, a spouse, or a stranger were just as likely to be answered falsely). And we can have a social agreement to tell the truth only if most people tell the truth most of the time. So unless most people tell the truth most of the time, lying is impossible. Thus, the liar is a kind of parasite or freeloader. He obtains something for himself, the chance to deceive you, by shirking his part in a common duty, that is, telling the truth. The liar achieves this advantage only if other people forgo the advantages of lying in favor of telling the truth.

From the principle of universality, thus, it follows that engineers must show great concern for truth and honesty. Only in extraordinary circumstances is it ethical to lie.

Example 11: Promising. We could not get on as we do without promising: promises are central to marriage and most business transactions, including employment ("If you work in my lab, I will pay you so much at the end of the month"). A promise allows me to get something from you. You mow my lawn now, because I promise to pay you when you finish. You certainly would not mow my lawn if you expect I will not keep my promise. So if people in our society generally fail to keep their promises, my saying "I promise to pay you ten dollars if you mow my lawn" means nothing, and I will not have my lawn mowed. Promising works only if most people keep their promises. The person who breaks his promises is thus a parasite—he is able to get something from you for nothing by exploiting the fact that most people keep their promises.

It follows from the principle of universality, then, that engineers must place a high value on keeping their promises. The principle of universality does not tell us that you should never break a promise. While you ought to keep your promises, it would be more important to save a drowning person than to keep your promise to me to be on time for my dinner party. Thus, you ought to stop to rescue the drowning person even if that makes you late to my party. So there are times when a promise cannot or should not be kept because keeping the promise would violate some other value or duty. However, the importance of keeping promises means that (1) promises should not be made lightly, and you should try to avoid making promises you might not be able to keep; (2) only a strong duty or value can outweigh your duty to keep a promise; and (3) when a promise cannot be kept, you owe the promisee something. Suppose I promise to go with Smith to the opera and later find I cannot keep my promise. I let Smith down. In response I should make every feasible attempt to make it up to Smith. Perhaps we can go to the ballet. Perhaps I can go with her to the next opera. At the very least I owe her an apology and an explanation. (See Case 24 later in this chapter.)

Example 12: Paying taxes. No one who is employed or has a business can function in our society without the benefits that tax dollars bring. The tax dodger obtains the benefit of taxes (schools, roads, etc.) for nothing because he shirks a duty that most people perform. Thus, engineers must not engage in dubious transactions for the purpose of avoiding taxes.

Remember that principles are only sources that must be weighed against other, conflicting sources. Two factors limit the principle of universality.

First, minor obligations must be subordinated to more pressing ones. The principle of universality says you have a duty to keep your promises. How pressing this duty is depends on the nature and importance of the promise: the more formal and solemn the promise and the more harmful the consequences of breaking the promise, the more pressing is the obligation to keep the promise. (An offhand promise to be on time to my dinner party is less pressing than a legal contract to be my bodyguard.) The obligation to keep a promise must be weighed against the moral and physical harm of keeping it. If keeping a promise means doing something immoral (e.g., keeping a promise to kill someone) or means allowing someone to die or come to harm, then there is a strong reason to break the promise.

Example 13: You promise a coworker that you will keep confidential what he is about to tell you. He tells you he is going to falsify safety figures for a nuclear power plant. The harm of keeping the promise is potentially widespread and deep, and keeping silent about it is immoral. The duty to prevent an unsafe plant from being constructed is more pressing than the duty to keep your promise to your coworker.

Second, duties may be allocated. For example, we all

need protection against fire. Am I being a parasite if I do not become a volunteer firefighter? No, because duties such as firefighting and cleaning the streets may be allocated: I may do my part by paying taxes to support a professional fire department or by doing some other form of volunteer work (you fight fires, I will help the sick). This is why it is not wrong to become a physician: social tasks such as planting crops, building roads, healing the sick, and singing opera are allocated to different individuals. Allocation is only an acceptable solution as long as the allocated tasks are being properly performed. When no one is doing an allocated task properly, we must take responsibility, individually or collectively.

Example 14: Although engineers are responsible for the safety of the projects in which they are engaged, no one can oversee and guarantee the safety of every aspect of a project. Thus, allocation of safety aspects to different teams or individuals is permissible. However, if an engineer becomes aware that some safety aspect is not being properly addressed by the team or person in her firm responsible for that aspect, she may not ignore it by saying ''That's not my area.''

Moral Precedents

The case study method, which is often used in business and law schools, also proves useful in ethical thinking: looking at other cases often gives us some guidance in making our own decisions. Three kinds of examples serve particularly well: (1) precedents, that is, clear or paradigmatic examples of good moral decisions we can try to emulate, (2) hard cases that raise tough questions and encourage us to reexamine our assumptions, and (3) pure (perhaps imaginary) cases that serve as good subjects for the "ethics lab."

Precedents are highly regarded persons, decisions, systems or institutions after which we want to model ourselves. For example, an engineer who has to make a tough moral decision might ask himself "How would X handle this?" where X is someone he respects and admires. Similarly, a supervisor might better understand how to balance patience and firmness by looking at the way Y, an outstanding supervisor, treats her employees. Precedents and principles work together: examples help make clear what principles mean and how to apply them, while principles help us see what is morally significant about past decisions.

Hard cases get us thinking about the issues and keep us from becoming too rigid and inflexible. For example, suppose your aunt is very near death but is of clear and sound mind. Her son has just been killed in an automobile accident. She asks you, "How's my son?" Should you tell her the truth and make her last hours miserable, or should you lie to her? Thinking about a case like this helps us see the tensions between honesty and promoting good consequences and may cast light on how we should treat other situations where being honest would produce bad consequences.

Pure cases play the same role in ethics that laboratory experiments play in science. In real life, it is difficult to isolate all the relevant factors. Thus, creating an artificially controlled environment sometimes proves useful. The same is true in ethics. The "hard case" above is not a pure case, since lying might also produce bad consequences—the dying aunt might be hurt that her son is not visiting her, or she may discover the truth and be hurt that you lied to her. So it is sometimes useful to invent a pure case of conflict between honesty and avoiding bad consequences. Again, in real life, few competent employees wholly lack personal integrity, and few employees with much personal integrity are highly incompetent. If you want to decide whether competence or personal integrity is more important in a given situation, you might imagine a highly competent scoundrel and an inept saint and ask which you would rather have working for you in that situation. This helps tell you, for that situation, which of the two is more important.

The Golden Rule

The Golden Rule is not really a rule at all, or at least not a viable one. Rather, it is an important technique of moral thinking, a guiding idea.

Sometimes applying the Golden Rule gives the wrong results: counterexamples to the rule ''Always treat others as you would wish to be treated'' are easy to invent. First, people differ and do not always want to be treated in the same way. For example, if I had a terminal disease, I would want to be told, and I would be quite angry if I later learned that the truth had been kept from me. So the Golden Rule seems to demand that I tell terminally ill patients of their condition, since that is how I would wish to be treated. However, suppose my aunt does not want to be told of her condition, and it may be best for her not to be told. Must I tell her she is dying, just because I would want to be told?

Second, it is sometimes wrong to treat people the way they want to be treated. For example, consider a student who fails a course because he never came to class and had no understanding of the material. The Golden Rule requires that the professor give that student an undeserved "A" because the professor, like most people, would rather get an undeserved "A" than an "F." Yet clearly it is wrong for the professor to give the student an undeserved "A."[30]

I suggest that we view the Golden Rule not as a rule but as a way of reminding ourselves of two important things. First, to understand the meaning of our actions, we must think about how they affect others. What is it like to be on the other end of what I am about to do? How would I feel if somebody did that to me? Thinking about what it would be like to be in the other person's shoes is an important part of understanding the moral character of what you are doing. Second, we must take very seriously the way we affect others. That is, the results of our "thought experiment" are important.

Illustrating Case

Case 21: Jones works very hard on a project. You are Jones' superior. You put the finishing touches on the project and pass it along to your supervisor, M, who assumes that most of the work is your own and praises you for the great job you did.

Discussion: You might be tempted to allow M to continue thinking that the credit belongs to you. But the Golden Rule tells you two things. First, it says, place yourself (using your imagination) in Jones' shoes: how would you feel if someone did that to you? You realize that you would be upset about not getting the credit you are due. Second, the Golden Rule tells you to take seriously the injustice to Jones that you are creating. So the Golden Rule gives you a strong reason to tell M that Jones did most of the work.

Personal Values and the Good Life

Since ethics is, at heart, about what is worthwhile and good in life, one basic source of ethical decision making is a vision of the good life, a sense of what kind of life is worth living and striving for. Having such a vision is a key not only to ethical decision making, but also to living well. People often do stupid things because they do not think about what truly matters. No one really thinks that the most important thing in life, the thing worth risking everything else for, is not letting anyone get ahead of you.[31] Yet we often see people on highways risking their lives to prevent others' cars from getting ahead of them.

Thinking about what really matters in life may change how you act, what you feel, and how you make ethical decisions. If you come to see that participating in a family is one of the really important things in life, you will spend more time with your family, and you will regard going to a PTA meeting not as an annoying distraction but as part of what really matters to you. If you come to see personal integrity as more important to a good life than consumer goods, you will be unwilling to lie to a prospective buyer of your used car about the fact that it tends to stall on cold mornings, because being a person of integrity is more important than the new couch you would buy with the extra money.

Closely related to a vision of the good life is a set of values, of those things we think are important for their own sake. Someone who values honesty not only wants to be honest, but also appreciates honesty in others. And he will help and encourage others to be honest. For example, he would want to provide an incentive for employees with a drug problem to come forward, perhaps by establishing a program in which those employees who admit to a drug problem are treated at company expense, while their job is kept open for them upon successful completion of the program. Similarly, a dedicated engineer and a great tennis player may both place a high value on excellence for its own sake. They may care less about the fame or money or success they derive from their work than they do about excellence as such. Therefore, they take delight in the skill of an opponent or rival and want to improve not only their own work, but the achievement level of the profession as a whole. Again, if I value the search for knowledge, I will not fudge the data in a scientific paper for presentation, even though presenting the tainted paper would further my career.

When to Break the Rules

One important and difficult ethical question professionals often have to face is "When should I break the rules?" When should an engineer not "work through channels"? When should a judge overlook a legal technicality? When should a professor make an exception to the rules for a student? When should a physician deceive a patient for his or her own good (by, for example, prescribing a placebo)?

When should an editor not print a newsworthy story? These questions have no simple answer, but certain considerations help guide professionals in answering them.

Theory

We might begin by asking "Why have rules at all?" There are three reasons for following rules: the need for reasonable expectations, fairness, and the need for rule-governed practices.

Reason 1: The need for reasonable expectations. Rules help us know what to expect, and people generally need to know what to expect and to be able to count on their expectations. Attorneys cannot prepare their cases in a reasonable way unless they know how the court will proceed, what it will admit as evidence, and so forth. So unless the court follows clear rules of evidence and procedure, attorneys cannot adequately represent their clients. Rules, in short, allow us to anticipate what will happen in life, so that we may form reasonable plans, engage in long-term projects, and so forth.

Reason 2: Fairness. Rules help ensure that like cases are treated alike. The rules governing the earning of merit badges in the Boy Scouts prevent John, who can only tie a half-hitch knot, from getting a knot-tying badge denied to Jim, who can tie both half-hitch and slip knots.

Reason 3: The need for rule-governed practices. Much of our lives depends on rule-governed practices, that is, social activities defined by a set of well-understood rules.[32] Chess, courtroom trials, square dancing, company audits, and political elections are rule-governed practices. So is baseball. I can swing a bat and throw a baseball just to "loosen up," or to practice, or because I like the feel of a bat in my hands. That is not playing baseball. My friends and I are playing baseball when we follow the rules about when to bat, when a run is scored, when a batter is out, and so forth. If you do not observe those rules, you are not playing baseball.[33]

Most professions are also rule-governed practices. Not everyone who makes people healthier is a physician: the role of the physician is spelled out by certain rules and norms, and only by following those rules and norms is one acting as a physician. There are many ways to teach, but only those who follow certain norms and rules about classes, lectures, discussions, grades, and so forth are professors. (Gandhi, for example, was in many ways a powerful teacher. But he was not a professor.) The same is true of engineers, judges, attorneys, and journalists. So one should generally follow the rules of engineering, judging, and so forth, because (1) unless one follows those rules one is not being an engineer or a judge, and (2) society benefits from having engineers and judges. That is, the profession as a whole is a useful one, and the profession exists only when its members follow the rules of the profession.[34]

Illustrating Examples

Example 15: Late in the season, the Cubs lead the Dodgers by one run in the eighth inning. The Dodgers are in contention for the division title, while the Cubs are in last place. The Cubs have a runner on third base. The Cubs' batter lifts a fly to shallow right field. The runner tags and races home, preceding by a fraction of a second the throw from right field. According to the rules of baseball, the runner is safe, and the Cubs score a run. One can imagine the Dodgers' manager arguing that it would be more useful to call the runner out, because this would make the game and the pennant race closer, providing more pleasure for the fans, which, after all, is the point of baseball.

We should all agree that the umpire should be unmoved by this argument because baseball is a rule-governed activity: you cannot have professional baseball if umpires bend the rules to make the game more exciting. The integrity of the rules is the backbone of the sport: it is what makes baseball a major league sport and not something else. True, the fans might have more pleasure if this particular call did not follow the rules. But for baseball to be a real sport the rules must be followed, and baseball as a sport gives a lot of pleasure.

Example 16: Because of a technicality regarding search and seizure procedures, evidence proving beyond a doubt that Green murdered his landlord is ruled inadmissible, thus permitting Green to go free. This may seem unfair at first glance, but the rule of law dictated that Green be set free. We do not have a system of law if judges feel free to bend the rules whenever the rules would let a murderer go free. If judges are free to bend the rules, then we have replaced the rule of law with the rule of individuals. The rule of law is a good thing, a better thing than the rule of individuals. Citizens need to know what to expect from their courts. So judges have a duty to obey the rules of law, even when following the rules in a particular case results in some unfairness.

Guidelines

Now that we understand why rules are important, we can determine when they should be broken. The three reasons for having rules do not apply equally to all situations. The first reason is the need for expectations. Clearly, not all expectations are equally important: it is more important to know when it is illegal to buy stock (insider trading laws) than to know when your dancing partner will do-si-do. The second reason is fairness. Here again, not every kind of unfairness is equally important, and not every case of treating people differently is equally unfair. The third reason is the importance of rule-governed practices. Notice first that not all activities are equally rule-governed. Professional baseball depends on strict adherence to the rules. A friendly game of tennis between husband and wife does not. The couple is not playing tennis if they follow no rules at all, but ignoring a few technicalities does not seem out of place, just as a legal contract is more rule-dependent than a casual promise to a friend would be. Second, not all rules are equally important to a practice. Third, some practices are more important and useful than others.

From these considerations, we can formulate four major questions to guide us in deciding whether to break a rule.

1. To what extent is the practice rule-dependent? Some practices are, by nature, ''looser'' than others. Professional sports needs strict rules, while the rules of etiquette can be fairly loose without making it impossible to be polite. So it is more important for baseball umpires to adhere strictly to the rules of baseball than it is for a host to adhere to the rules of etiquette. One key factor is the extent to which it is necessary for others to be able to anticipate precisely how the professional will act. For example, lawyers and therapists require their clients to divulge confidential information. Unless clients tell their attorneys and therapists very sensitive and personal information, their attorneys and therapists cannot help them. The very nature of legal representation and therapy means that clients must rely on the confidentiality of what they say. So it is crucial for clients to be able to anticipate when attorneys and therapists will reveal information confided to them during therapy or as part of preparing a defense. It is much less important for you as a guest to be able to anticipate precisely how your host will greet you when you walk in the door.

2. How central to the practice is this rule? There are several ways of assessing the centrality of a rule. First, to what extent would the practice be recognizable without this rule? Most practices have peripheral rules that can change without destroying the practice. In bridge, for example, whether ''honors'' scores fifty points or a hundred points is peripheral—if the rule about this were changed tomorrow, we would still think of the game as bridge. But a game in which reneging is allowed would not be bridge at all: the essence of the game, its fundamental strategies and logic, would be lost. Similarly, a minor technicality of procedure is peripheral to the rule of law, while convicting someone without a hearing strikes at the very roots of lawfulness. In short, breaking some rules has less effect upon the integrity of the practice than breaking others.

Another relevant question is ''How important to the practice is standardizing this aspect?'' For example, accounting would not be accounting without standard book-keeping practices, forms of ledger entry, and so forth. Following the rules about these matters is crucial to what makes accounting a profession. By contrast, a professor who uses good but unusual grading methods and teaching styles is still recognizably a professor—standardization of these things is not crucial to teaching's being a profession.

A third relevant question is "What kind of rule is it?" Of the first importance are the rules without which the practice could not exist, such as rules of confidentiality for attorneys and therapists, rules of evidence for courts, and so forth. Of second importance are rules governing the tone, setting, and public role of the profession, such as the rule that English barristers wear wigs. Least important are rules for ease of communication and cooperation, which may usually be broken without harm when all parties involved are comfortable with and understand the situation.

A final question in judging the centrality of a rule is "How does keeping the rule in this case relate to the point of the rule?" For example, the rules of confidentiality concerning audit accountants are meant to ensure that businesses can obtain accurate audits without having their legitimate business secrets revealed. The rules are not meant to protect fraud. So an audit accountant may have to break confidentiality to reveal a fraud, as long as legitimate business secrets are protected. (By contrast, the rules of attorney-client confidentiality do cover possible illegality, since the point of the rules is to enable clients to prepare a defense by discussing actions that might have been illegal.) Similarly, the rules of bidding are meant to promote fair commerce. If following the rule in a given case would undermine instead of promote fair commerce, this is a reason for breaking the rule (which must be weighed against the other reasons for not breaking the rule).

3. How does the value of the point or aim of the practice measure against the harm caused by following the rules? Not all practices are equally important. Baseball, whose purpose is to give pleasure, is less important than medicine, since health and life are more important than the sort of pleasure one gets from a baseball game. So if following the rules of baseball places people's lives in jeopardy, it is better to give up playing baseball than to follow the rules.

4. How unfair would it be to others if this case were treated differently? This question has two aspects. Would there be any real unfairness if not all cases are treated alike in this regard? For example, it is important that the success of a defendant's case does not depend on which judge tries the case. It would be unfair for defendants who get a "lenient" judge to be treated better than defendants who get a "strict" judge. Thus, a judge must hesitate before she bends the rules, even in the cause of justice, if she feels that other judges might not act as she does. The other aspect concerns appearances. How sensitive to the appearance of irregularity is the situation? In many cases the appearance of impropriety or favoritism is almost as bad as the actuality of it. This is especially true of positions of public trust, such as the judiciary. In general, strict uniformity is more important in situations of conflict than in situations of cooperation, in formal than in informal settings, and in public than in private settings.

These questions of fairness articulate factors that must be balanced one against another: the factors in favor of breaking the rule in this case must be weighed against the factors in favor of following the rule. For example, if breaking the rule would appear highly irregular in a situation of intense conflict, this would outweigh a small actual unfairness that would result if the rule were followed.

In general, rules should be followed unless the case for breaking them is very strong. Give the benefit of the doubt to following the rules. Also follow the rules if the reasons for breaking them are only slightly stronger than the reasons for following them.

Illustrating Cases

Case 22: Is it ethical to buy a product without an investigation or bidding process when the product is fairly good and, although there might be a better product (or equally good, cheaper product), the advantage gained by procuring the other product is probably minor, not worth the effort and cost of an investigation?

Discussion: The engineering profession cannot operate as it does without public trust: reliance in the strict probity and fairness of bidding and supplying procedures is a precondition for engineers to function as they do. Hence, engineers have an institutional duty of strict propriety in these matters. The rules of propriety here are central to the practice of engineering: to buy materials casually, haphazardly, or on the basis of friendship rather than through a clean-cut, rigorous, rational decision process would strike at the heart of engineering as a professional practice. It is important to the practice of engineering that bidding be reasonably standardized, in part because the interests of commerce (for both buyers and suppliers) is best served when suppliers can anticipate how buyers will go about making purchases. Moreover, the situation potentially involves conflict (because the firms involved in supplying and bidding on contracts are competitors), and so the appearance of impropriety is almost as damaging as actual impropriety. The legitimate gain in bending these rules, the avoidance of a brief bidding or investigation process, is minor.

Thus, there is a very strong case for strict adherence to rules of propriety: the engineer should institute a bidding or investigation process. In general, engineers should err in the direction of caution in giving or accepting anything that smacks of a favor or gift, in acquiring an interest in a supplier or potential contractor, and so forth. The rule of thumb is ''If there's any doubt, don't do it.''

Nevertheless, it is clearly silly to institute a bidding procedure before buying a single fifty-cent green pencil. Our four questions help us to see why this is so. Neither the possible saving to the buyer nor the possible profit made by the seller comes close to the cost and trouble of taking and submitting bids. There is no point to extending the rules of bidding to tiny purchases. Thus, keeping to the rules about bidding when buying one fifty-cent pencil seems to conflict with the point of the rules, which is to facilitate fair commerce. Rules about tiny purchases are peripheral rather than central. And, because only a few cents are involved, no real unfairness is involved, and this is not a situation of potential conflict in the way that major purchasing is.

Case 23: Making a minor ''adjustment'' to records would greatly simplify matters (for example, back-dating an order by one day would significantly simplify calculating taxes).

Discussion: The same considerations apply to bookkeeping procedures as to purchasing procedures. The legitimate use of such procedures depends upon reliance on their strict accuracy. Record keeping as a practice is highly rule-governed and demands strict adherence to rules—lax records serve little purpose. It is crucial to record keeping as a practice that records be standardized. Back-dating an order, however harmless it may appear, casts doubt on the very practice of dating orders, and without public trust in the accuracy of such matters a profession cannot function as it needs to. (For example, the Internal Revenue Service could not trust firms to do their own record keeping and would have to require such things as government-kept books, a practice that would be costly to the government, to engineers, and to customers.) Thus, there is an institutional duty of strict adherence to these rules and to avoiding any appearance of impropriety. Moreover, the benefit of bending the rule, namely, avoiding a complicated accounting procedure, is minor compared to the benefits conferred by the practice of strict record keeping.

Case 24: You are the head of the Civil Engineering Department of City N. You promise Washington, who wants to take a year's unpaid leave, that her job will be there for her when she returns. Meanwhile, the budget is severely cut. The best way of adjusting to the reduced budget includes eliminating Washington's job.

Discussion: Drawing upon the discussion of Example 11 (promising), two conflicting arguments could be made. The first argument goes as follows:

Promises should be kept.
You promised Washington her job would be kept for her.
_____

Therefore you should keep Washington's job.

The second argument centers on the duties of a public servant:

A civil servant should do what is in the best interests of the public. It is in the best interests of the public to eliminate Washington's job.
_____

Therefore you should eliminate Washington's job.

As in all cases in which moral factors pull in opposite directions, you must weigh, for this particular case, the importance of keeping your promise against the importance of best serving the public. If, for example, the hardship for Washington of losing her job would be severe but the gain in public service of cutting her job would be slight, then you should keep Washington's job. Another factor is the nature of the promise made to Washington. A casual promise is less binding than a solemn oath. To what extent can Washington reasonably rely upon the kind of promise you made to her?

PART THREE

Problems and Issues in Engineering

5

Honesty and Professionalism

Honesty and professionalism sometimes require that engineers make tough decisions. No one wants to blow the whistle on her own company, inform customers of the defects of the product she is trying to sell, turn down a promotion (when the job is beyond her competence), or censure her friends and colleagues. Good people are sometimes tempted to avoid taxes or red tape by taking a "shortcut"; modifying the records slightly often saves much work and money. Should one "give in" and "cook the books"? The material in this chapter will help you to make these decisions.

Whistleblowing

Although many companies and firms recognize that being unsafe or unethical generally does not pay off in the long run, it is unfortunately true that some companies or firms will try to cover up or ignore serious problems, such as unsafe products, violations of environmental law (such as illegal dumping of toxic waste), falsified test results, or discriminatory hiring and promotion. The concerned engineer's efforts to persuade the company to correct the problem may prove futile. If the problem seems serious enough, engineers may feel a need to "blow the whistle" on their company or firm by taking the problem directly to the client, the appropriate regulatory agency, or the press.[1] Nevertheless, loyalty to their firm or company, confidentiality, and the fear of reprisal all make engineers understandably reluctant to blow the whistle. The decision to blow the whistle is never an easy one. Whatever decision you make will leave you feeling uncomfortable, because whatever you do will involve betraying a loyalty. Whistleblowing always involves a conflict between loyalty to the company and loyalty to society and sometimes involves a conflict between moral duties such as honesty and fairness. Thus, every attempt should be made to address the problem within the company or in a way that does not harm the company. In some rare cases, this is impossible. So the ethical engineer needs some guidance about when whistleblowing is permissible and when whistleblowing is morally required. The following factors and remarks may help if you are ever in this situation.

Ronald Duska argues that whistleblowing is required when there is a clear harm to society, "it is the 'proximity' to the whistleblower that puts him in the position to report his company in the first place," there is some chance of succeeding, and no one else is more able to blow the whistle and more proximate.[2] Richard T. de George suggests that, because each of us is "morally obliged to prevent serious harm to others," whistleblowing is justifiable if the problem poses a serious harm to the public and all avenues within the company have been exhausted. Whistleblowing is required, says de George, if, in addition, the employee has documentation of the problem and the employee has good reason to believe that whistleblowing will bring about the necessary changes to safeguard the public.[3]

On one hand, five factors count in favor of whistleblowing. The duty to promote good consequences means that you should be prepared to take major steps to prevent catastrophic harm. The duty to leave the world no worse suggests that you have an obligation not to participate in activities that will leave the world significantly worse than you found it. The institutional duties of engineering as well as the values of engineering as a profession require putting a high premium on public safety and acting to ensure that public safety is not compromised. The principles of accountability require that you take feasible steps to ensure that your company does no wrong. The points mentioned in ''When to Fight a Battle'' in Chapter 4 suggest that if you are in a special position to know about or correct the harm, or if you are closely connected to the institution doing the wrong, then you have a special responsibility to do something about it.

On the other hand, three factors count against whistleblowing. The importance of loyalty toward the employer and of maintaining a community atmosphere of teamwork and mutual interest within the company intimates that you should not betray your loyalty to your company and coworkers. Treating others fairly means that you may not publicly accuse or take other harmful action against another person without hearing the other person's (or the company's) side and weighing the evidence very carefully. Whistleblowing often requires a breach of confidentiality. (For example, it is often impossible to document a danger without releasing company records, test results, or trade secrets.)

These factors must be weighed, and a compromise solution reached. For example, exhausting all in-house avenues before going public would take some account of loyalty to the firm and the importance of community and would also accommodate the need to hear the other person's side, all without severely compromising the five factors in favor of whistleblowing (except in the case of a pressing emergency). Thus, an employee should not blow the whistle without exhausting all in-house remedies: the employee must go the extra mile to deal with the problem within the company in a supportive and constructive way.

Nevertheless, the company cannot operate as a community if it is devious or immoral, and thus if the company spurns all of an engineer's many attempts to get it to address a well-documented, serious, and immoral danger it poses to society, the demands of loyalty and community become less relevant. That is, if the community atmosphere of the company cannot be restored until the harm is redressed, and if whistleblowing is the only way to redress it, then loyalty and community do not weigh very heavily against whistleblowing.

Violating confidentiality is particularly troubling, since the engineer came into possession of the information only because he was trusted to keep it confidential. Thus, in publicizing the information, he is violating a trust and breaking an implicit promise. (See the discussion of promising in "Universality" in Chapter 4.) The engineer faces a conflict, in other words, between keeping a promise and participating in making the world worse. One can resolve this conflict by asking, "Is the firm or company entitled to ask for such a promise on my part?" It is wrong to ask someone to promise to help you steal, and an unethical promise of that sort has no moral standing. (That is why, in contract law, immoral contracts are not enforceable.) Similarly, it is wrong to ask you to help cover up theft, embezzlement, or fraud. So, while the duty of confidentiality is very strong, it does not include covering up a crime. In general, releasing confidential information without your employer's consent is permissible only when every attempt has been made to obtain the employer's consent and it is absolutely necessary to document extreme and severe danger to the public, serious violations of the law, or grossly immoral conduct.

Finally, the whistleblower must realize that the personal consequences of whistleblowing are often severe. The whistleblower may well lose his or her job. Even whistleblower protection laws leave plenty of loopholes: the company can "reorganize" a department and eliminate the whistleblower's job in the process. It is difficult to prove that the reorganization was a form of retaliation and not a legitimate business decision. Even if the whistleblower keeps her job, she may suffer harassment on the job through unwelcome transfers or working conditions ("Welcome to your new office in the boiler room," or "We need you in our Antarctica office"). When a company transfers an engineer to a remote location, it is hard to prove that the transfer was a form of retaliation rather than a legitimate business judgment.

Moreover, future employers are often wary of hiring someone who blew the whistle. Fortunately, as more companies and firms actively seek ethically minded engineers, "going public" may not mean "the kiss of death." After all, suppose you are the head of a large research and development department. You are an ethical person and would not tolerate falsified test results. Unfortunately, you cannot personally oversee the integrity of every aspect of every project. Would you rather hire an engineer who will give in to project leader N's demand to falsify results or an engineer who would speak up and come to you with the problem? So, provided the employee can show you that he made every attempt to work within the company before blowing the whistle and that the problem involved was well-documented, real, and serious, you would want him working for you. (Remember that, because you are ethical, you know that the employee would not need to go public if he came to you with a well-documented, serious problem.)

Nonetheless, life is not easy for the whistleblower. Apart from being fired or harassed, she can expect to be publicly attacked, to have her motives, her personal life, and her professional competence questioned in the media. The potential whistleblower should thus ask herself whether her motives and her competence can withstand this kind of scrutiny, whether she and her family have the ability to weather the storm, and whether her documentation will stand up to a determined attack.

The whistleblower, therefore, must consider the issues very carefully before going public. Which questions she must ask herself depends on the situation. Suppose an engineer is actively involved in an unsafe project. Then she must ask herself whether she can live with being an accomplice. After all, if you are helping to build an unsafe nuclear power plant and you do not speak out, you must recognize that in the event of a serious accident, you are personally responsible for the death and suffering that ensues. Suppose the engineer is tempted simply to quit instead of going public. Then she must ask herself whether this is something she can walk away from (she must weigh the factors mentioned in "When to Fight a Battle" in Chapter 4). After all, the problem remains even if she leaves the company or firm. In the case of an unsafe reactor, the danger is likely, severe, and widespread; she is in a special position to know about the problem; and her speaking out is likely to lead to change. Can she live with herself after a lethal accident if she did not speak out but simply changed jobs? So she must ask herself, "Is there a neutral option?" "How bad is it?" (morally and in terms of the likelihood, severity, and number of people affected by the risk) and "How directly am I involved?" (That is, she must ask, "Am I involved in the infraction?" "Am I closely tied to the infracting organization?" "Am I in a special position to know about or correct the problem?" and "Would doing nothing compromise doing my job faithfully?")

Suppose she is tempted to pass on the information anonymously. Then she must ask herself whether an anonymous "leak" would be effective in solving the problem and whether the leak would really remain anonymous. The answer to both questions is often "no." Sometimes leaking the problem without providing documentation or testimony would not result in the problem's being corrected. If you do provide the documentation, it may be easy for the company to figure out who leaked it. Sometimes, thus, leaking the information anonymously is simply not a viable solution.

Finally, she needs to ask herself how vulnerable she is: "Can I afford to go public?" The answers to these questions are, of course, connected. If the problem is bad enough, you are directly involved, your speaking up would correct the problem, and no one else will speak up, then you have to be prepared to bear any cost, even going to prison if necessary.

If the engineer does decide to do something about the problem, she must make every feasible attempt to work within the company, and she must document everything (both the problem itself and her attempts to resolve the problem within the company). Leaving a paper trail is often the key to successful whistleblowing.

Fortunately, whistleblowing situations can often be avoided. First, choose your employer judiciously. Do not work for unethical firms or companies. Second, deal with potential problem situations early. If you notice a tendency to cut corners about minor matters, deal with it before a major catastrophe looms. If you think there may be safety or construction irregularities in a project, check it out and deal with it before deadlines approach and correcting the problem would cost the company dearly. The earlier you deal with a problem, the easier it is to resolve it, both for you and for your company. Third, before any problems arise, suggest that your firm or company establish troubleshooting mechanisms for dealing with such problems. Prevention is generally the best way of dealing with whistleblowing. As Ron Westrum notes, "[W]histleblowing is essentially a last-ditch measure. It should be used when everything else has failed. It cannot solve the problems of most organizations."[4] Westrum quotes Samuel Florman's remark that "a system that relies on heroism is neither stable nor efficient."[5] Instead, Westrum recommends that companies establish troubleshooting mechanisms such as ombudspersons.

Illustrating Cases

Case 25: Engineer Alomar of Z consultants is asked to sample the outflow from Y company's plant into a river used for drinking water. The Department of Environmental Quality chose the sampling site. Alomar discovers that the sampling site is actually upstream of the main point of discharge. Although samples taken at the selected site are uniformly under the limit, samples taken from below the main point of discharge indicate an average of 0.020 milligrams per liter of cadmium, well above the legal limit. Alomar notifies both the head of Z consultants and the president of Y company. Both order Alomar to remain silent about what he has discovered.

Discussion: Recall from Chapter 3 that cadmium, which accumulates in the kidneys, is linked to kidney disease and high blood pressure and remains in the body a long time (it has a half-life of ten to thirty years). The factors discussed under "Safety" in Chapter 3 suggest that Alomar should speak up. The risk involved is serious (kidney disease), widespread (it applies to everyone who drinks the water), and fairly likely. The danger to the public is not voluntarily undertaken, nor is the public aware of the risk. The individuals taking the risk are not, in general, those receiving the benefit. One would not want one's family to undergo the risk of drinking cadmium-laden water for these benefits, and, if Alomar ignores the problem, he is not being a good trustee of the public welfare. Moreover, the community can take steps to protect itself if the danger from cadmium pollution is known, which makes publicizing the risk all the more important. In addition, dumping dangerous doses of cadmium into a river hardly constitutes acting in partnership with nature, and if Alomar does not speak up, he is participating in making the world a worse place than he found it. Alomar has already done everything feasible to work within the company. If he remains silent, he becomes an accomplice. Drawing on the factors mentioned in ''When to Fight a Battle'' in Chapter 4, we find that Alomar is directly involved, that remaining silent does interfere with doing his job properly, and that the infraction is serious. This is not a problem Alomar may walk away from, since he is deeply involved, has documentable evidence of a serious harm, and is in a special position to know about and do something about the danger.

Of course, speaking up would conflict with loyalty to the client. However, the point of the duty of loyalty is to protect the legitimate interests of a client, and the client's interest in getting away with causing kidney disease is not a legitimate interest that deserves protection. Moreover, unlike some of the more controversial cases of whistleblowing, Alomar's speaking out does not require him to break confidentiality, since the site of the discharge is not a trade secret. In any case, not speaking up would constitute fraud, and promises that require fraud are not binding, since the point of promising is not undermined by refusing to keep promises that constitute committing fraud (see "When to Break the Rules" in Chapter 4).

Thus, Alomar should document everything carefully and then inform the Department of Environmental Quality (DEQ) of the problem in a way that does minimal harm to Z consultants. If DEQ does not change the sampling site, Alomar must consider taking the problem to the governor or going public.[6]

Case 26: A company, in order to remain competitive, instructs an engineer in its employ to "go easy" on a safety assessment of a procedure or product. The engineer believes the product or procedure may jeopardize workers' safety but also believes that no cost-effective way of resolving the problem exists. How should the matter be handled?

Case 27: (Based on the Bay Area Rapid Transit case.) Your company is responsible for installing an expensive automated subway system. You are aware that (1) the automatic train control is unsafely designed, (2) contractors building the system are inadequately monitored, (3) the software designed to run the system exhibits continual problems, and (4) plans for training operators and performing safety tests before public use of the system are inadequate. You write a series of memos about these problems to your employers, including your immediate supervisors and two higher levels of management. No action is taken. (Note: In the case of the Bay Area Rapid Transit system, the engineers who wrote to the board of directors of the city's mass transit system were eventually fired. Problems did plague the system when it became operational: the computers were prone to losing sight of trains temporarily, a crystal oscillator malfunctioned, and on October 2, 1972, a train hit a sandpile.[7])

Consider these possibilities:

1. Although you work for the company, you are not specifically assigned to monitor the safety of this project.
2. You decide to go outside of normal channels and contact the board of directors of the city's mass transit system. They wish you to provide them with signed documentation of the problem, to be released to the press. Alternatively, the board does not dispute your conclusions but for political reasons decides to take no action.
3. You are told by your supervisor to keep your concerns to yourself.

Case 28: On January 28, 1986, the space shuttle Challenger exploded, killing six astronauts and a schoolteacher. Dr. James C. Fletcher, head of the National Aeronautics and Space Administration (NASA) in 1973, worked hard to have the contract awarded to Morton Thiokol, which had strong backing by the Church of Latter-day Saints and Utah state officials. (Dr. Fletcher belonged to the Latter-day Saints and was a member of Pro-Utah, a Utah state lobbying organization.) The decision to use a segmented booster was due, in part, to the awarding of the contract to Morton Thiokol, which was rated fourth, behind Aerojet General, which proposed to make the booster from a single tube. Authority to oversee the project was transferred from Lewis Research Center to Marshall Space Flight Center. Between 1970 and 1985, the number of quality control personnel at Marshall was reduced from 615 to 88. Roger Boisjoly was the engineer responsible for the design of the booster segment joints. Early experiments showed that low temperature affected the seals.

In 1985 Boisjoly wrote a memorandum to Morton Thiokol management, insisting that this problem with the seals could result in "catastrophe." On January 27, in a teleconference with NASA and Morton Thiokol management, Boisjoly urged that, due to the low temperature, the launch be delayed. At first Morton Thiokol agreed with Boisjoly. However, NASA officials asked Morton Thiokol to reconsider. Pressure from management led Robert Lund, vice-president of engineering at Morton Thiokol, to agree to the launch.[8] (In later remarks, Roger Boisjoly said he would not sign off on anything he would not want his wife and children to use.)[9]

Case 29: The cargo hold and passenger cabin of the DC-10 are both pressurized at high altitudes.[10] If a midair collision, explosion, or sabotage causes a hole in the fuselage, resulting in either compartment being depressurized, or if the cargo door should open midflight, the cabin floor separating the compartments will buckle, as it is not designed to withstand the force of the pressure differential. (Minimizing weight is a key design goal.) Since hydraulic control lines run through the cabin floor, serious buckling results in loss of control of the airplane.

The problem was noted during the design of the DC-10, resulting in what Daniel Applegate, director of product engineering for Convair, later called "Band-Aid" remedies that did not solve the problem. On June 12, 1972, the cargo door problem nearly resulted in a crash with sixty-seven passengers aboard. This prompted Applegate to write a memorandum to his superiors predicting that a certain number of DC-10 cargo doors will come open, resulting in the loss of the airplane. In particular, Applegate noted that a design flaw makes it possible for the crew to think the cargo door was securely latched when the lock pins were not fully engaged. Convair decided to suppress the memo rather than pass it on to McDonnell Douglas, and Convair reached an agreement with the Federal Aviation Administration: on the basis of Convair's promise that the problem would be rectified, the agency would take no action. Convair did make some alternations, none of them adequate. It should be noted that McDonnell Douglas was experiencing financial difficulty and felt that delay in producing the DC-10 might jeopardize the existence of the company. Convair and McDonnell Douglas were already disputing how costs of design changes were to be apportioned between the companies, and Convair did not wish to risk footing the bill for expensive changes. What, if anything, should Applegate do? (Note: In 1974 the cargo door of a DC-10 opened midflight. All 346 people on board were killed.)

Case 30: A. Ernest Fitzgerald, a cost analyst for the U.S. Air Force, found over a billion dollars' worth of cost overruns on Lockheed's C-5A Galaxy transport. He informed William Proxmire's senate committee of the problem. Although Fitzgerald had previously been given awards for saving the government money, he was investigated. After the investigation of Fitzgerald unearthed no improprieties, he was sent to work on bowling alleys in Thailand. Eventually his position was eliminated, and Fitzgerald found himself blacklisted. He remained unemployed for four years, and he was not "fully reinstated" for thirteen years.[11]

Case 31: Mechanical engineer Carl Houston, of Stone and Webster, inspected the welding operation for a nuclear power plant under construction in Surry, Virginia. He discovered improper choice of electrodes, omission of oven drying, and underqualification of welders. Houston reported his findings to the manager and to Stone and Webster. Nothing was done to modify welding practices. Houston eventually notified Virginia Electric and Power Corporation, the reactor manufacturer, the Atomic Energy Commission, the governor of Virginia, the Virginia Department of Labor, and two U.S. senators. Eventually, the Atomic Energy Commission and a consulting firm engaged by Virginia Electric and Power confirmed Houston's charges. The license of the Surry plant was restricted, and the inspection rate of the plant was increased.[12]

Competence

Engineers have an institutional duty of competence, since the public places its trust in the competence of engineers. Competence is also a key component of professionalism generally and, more specifically, a value of the engineering profession (excellence and clean decision making are impossible without competence). Moreover, incompetent engineering endangers public safety, leads to bad consequences, and harms the firm or company.

Accordingly, engineers have a twofold duty. They must make every effort to be as competent as possible, and they should never undertake a task or responsibility beyond their competence. The first duty means that engineering is a life-long learning experience. Engineers should strive to increase their knowledge and skills. This may include reading trade and professional books and journals; attending professional meetings, workshops, and seminars; taking additional courses or other training; and making the most of work opportunities. Ask questions, try to understand all the decisions pertinent to your project, speak to colleagues about what they are doing, try new things. Another consequence of this duty is that you must make every effort to be at your best. Avoid coming to work tired. Prevent personal troubles from interfering with your work. Take care of your health, both mental and physical. Exercise, relaxation, proper diet, a good attitude, and plenty of mental stimulation are all essential to functioning at your best.

The second duty means that engineers must know and be candid about their own limitations. You should never be afraid to say ''I don't know'' and never be too proud to look up information about which you are not certain. When you are asked to do tasks beyond your abilities, you should speak up. When you need assistance, ask for it.

Illustrating Case

Case 32: You are a senior chemical engineer. The project you were supervising has just been completed. The engineer in charge of mechanical safety for a plant dies suddenly. Because the company is experiencing a temporary financial squeeze, it does not want to hire a new supervisor or promote anyone. You are therefore asked to assume the vacated position temporarily, until the financial picture improves or another senior engineer becomes available. Although you had some courses dealing with mechanical safety in college, your work over the last fifteen years has been in a different area, and you do not feel competent to assume the position. How should you handle the matter?

The Role of Professional Societies

Although most engineering disciplines have professional societies, to date the societies have had little effect upon the practice of the profession. Stephen Unger suggests that professional societies in engineering can play a role similar to that played in higher education by the American Association of University Professors (AAUP). According to Unger, AAUP censure is effective as a deterrent because "the general reputation that the Association has acquired for conducting careful investigations and publishing accurate and fair reports" means that top academics who have a choice may avoid censured institutions, and because "the principles espoused by the AAUP have been accepted widely enough . . . so that conformity to them has become the norm."[13] Unger suggests that similar factors apply to engineering because "competition for top notch engineers is keen" and, since many purchasers are engineers, censure may cost a company sales.[14]

Unfortunately, Unger overlooks a few flaws in this analogy. First, while companies support themselves primarily by profitably producing, universities support themselves largely through prestige and reputation: since tuition rarely covers more than half the cost of running the university, donations from private or state sources are the key to fiscal health. Moral censure of an academically strong school affects donations more than moral censure of a competitive company affects sales because companies choose suppliers mostly on the basis of cost and quality, while individuals give donations mostly because of the worthiness of the project. Thus, universities are more financially vulnerable to moral censure than are companies.

Second, the cost to universities of abiding by AAUP rules is generally much less than the cost to companies of ethical behavior. A professor's salary runs from twenty thousand dollars to seventy thousand dollars a year. The cost to a company of acting ethically may run in the millions of dollars. Thus, it is financially foolish for a university to risk AAUP censure to save on a few professors' salaries, while it may often appear cost-beneficial to companies to risk censure by the Institute of Electrical and Electronics Engineers (IEEE).

Nonetheless, it is true that companies often spend millions of dollars in public relations and might well hesitate to jeopardize that effort by being censured. If, in addition, IEEE censure acts as a warning bell to legislators and regulators, the effects of censure may be adequate to serve as a significant deterrent.

For professional engineering societies to have a significant impact on corporate ethics, three changes must occur in the way these societies approach ethics investigations: they must (1) change the nature of the issues on which they take action, (2) change the nature of the investigative procedure, and (3) change the kind of sanctions taken when fault is found. To date, censure or disciplinary action by professional societies has centered on infractions of codes of ethics, often involving technicalities rather than real harm or moral transgression. On August 8, 1989, the

Louisiana State Board of Registration for Professional Engineers took action against a registered professional engineer because the firm for which he worked provided engineering services without being registered. The company stated that the violation was the result of an oversight and agreed to a five-hundred-dollar fine and a public reprimand.[15] Censure for such an oversight, in violation of professional codes of conduct, would carry little moral onus, thus weakening the effect of censure. Unfortunately, since professional codes must be quite general to gain acceptance, many of the most crucial moral issues are either untouched by or not clearly settled by professional codes.

In addition, ethics boards typically review a case after the relevant decisions have been made. They do not, as a rule, become involved in questions in progress, when their assistance and moral force would be most beneficial. As Unger points out, conflicts can often be settled at an early stage, before harm is done either to individuals or to the company's reputation.

Finally, formal announcement of censure is not adequate. Unger suggests that professional societies institute an honor roll, grant awards, provide legal defense services, make pensions portable, and give support in the job market. This last suggestion deserves additional comment. Members of the society ought to make a special effort and commitment to hire engineers found by the society to be unjustly fired. This commitment may take the form of a special placement service for victims of unethical practices. This would benefit not only the fired engineers but also the companies who hire them, since, in most cases, the person they are hiring has proven that he or she is an ethical individual. In addition, I suggest that professional societies should make more of an effort to publicize their findings. A one-time statement of censure in a professional journal counts little against the persistent national advertising of the company. Notices of censure mailed to the company's major purchasers and a list of censured companies mailed to all graduating engineering students would have a more powerful effect.

Thus, I am suggesting that professional societies must be a more active force for good in all stages of an ethical problem. They must actively participate in resolving ethics problems, preferably as early as possible. They must be willing to make complex moral judgments, giving advice and acting as arbitrators. This means that ethics boards must distinguish between difficult cases in which they give advice and clear cases in which they make a ruling. Rulings should, as much as possible, be prospective rather than retrospective, since the main goal is to suggest remedies rather than censure past behavior. Censure should be reserved for companies, firms, and engineers who refuse to accept rulings: individuals should be given a chance to rectify problems before being condemned. However, sterner measures should be taken against recalcitrant companies and individuals who persist in unethical behavior despite the ethics boards' rulings.

Keeping Accurate Records and Obeying the Law

Three key rules apply to record keeping and following regulations. First, engineers must not falsify records or break the law. Second, engineers should be faithful to the spirit as well as to the letter of the law and should not seek loopholes to circumvent either the law or sound record-keeping principles. Third, engineers must be scrupulous in avoiding the appearance of impropriety. Never say or write anything you would not wish to explain in court.

Engineers must not falsify records because records are useful only if others can depend on their strict accuracy. Without public trust in the accuracy of records, engineering could not function as a profession. The considerations mentioned in ''When to Break the Rules'' in Chapter 4 more fully explain why records, especially records that have a legal use or status, may not be altered or falsified.

The case for obeying the law is even stronger than for keeping accurate records. The law represents the moral values of the community, as well the community's decisions about matters that affect it. When an engineer breaks the law, he is denying the public the ability to decide about its own future, thus violating the rights of citizens. The law also constitutes the ground rules by which business is to be carried out. The considerations mentioned in ''When to Break the Rules'' in Chapter 4 indicate that, since business is competitive and public, those rules must be respected. Moreover, no company can survive unless people generally obey the law. No corporation could operate without a framework of laws to protect its property, without courts to uphold its contracts, or without the roads, sewers, and financial system established by the community through its government. Thus, when a company breaks the law, it violates the principle of universality. (That is, a law-breaking company freeloads upon others that are obeying the law.) It cheats the community without whose services the company could not survive.

It is equally important to observe the *spirit* of laws or regulations. Because laws and record keeping serve a valid purpose, it is generally wrong to defeat that purpose by using loopholes to circumvent the spirit of the law or to create dubious or misleading records. In addition, using loopholes often violates the principle of universality. For example, the government passes pollution control laws and regulations to protect the health and environment of its citizens. If all companies use a legal loophole to pollute beyond tolerable limits, the government will simply rewrite the laws and regulations. If company A pollutes by exploiting the loophole, while companies B and C do not, then A is freeloading on B's and C's compliance with the spirit of the law. Similarly, using misleading record-keeping techniques freeloads on those companies that keep honest records, for if all companies used "creative record keeping," no one would trust any company's records.

Finally, the mere appearance of irregularity can cause harm, even when the letter and spirit of laws and regulations have not been violated. In particular, common sense dictates that you should be careful about what you say or write. Engineers should be aware that there is no such thing as a private comment or memo. Everything you say or write could conceivably wind up in court. Furthermore, every remark you make at a party, a church or social function, or while standing in line, reflects on your firm or company: people who know you work for company P will judge company P in the light of what you say. Think of yourself as an ambassador for your company, because in an important sense you represent the company in everything you do or say.

You should be particularly careful in anything touching on sensitive matters, such as antitrust, discrimination, and regulatory laws. Give extra thought to every remark or memorandum that might be construed as expressing a bias concerning race, gender, national origin, sexual orientation, or religion. Avoid using terms or phrases that might suggest either power to control or collusion in controlling market factors. Avoid using terms or phrases that might suggest less than strict and voluntary compliance with laws and regulations.

Consulting versus Adversarial Sales

Because many engineers become involved in the sale of their company's product, it is worth mentioning some special problems that sales engineers face. Buyers and sellers can build one of two possible sales relationships: the buyer and seller can be adversaries, or the seller can act as a consultant to the buyer. In adversarial sales, the buyer and the seller view themselves as opponents. Each is out for his own advantage at the expense of the other. They place no trust in each other and take no responsibility for meeting the other's needs. They are not interested in fairness or honesty, and they will take any advantage, however unfair or dishonorable, that the law permits. In consulting sales, by contrast, the seller acts as a consultant to the buyer, trying to figure out how the seller's company can best meet the buyer's needs. He invites the trust of the buyer, with the understanding that he and his company will not abuse that trust. In short, the sales engineer can present himself either as an adversary, proclaiming "Let the buyer beware," or as a trustworthy advisor.

While adversarial sales may be appropriate to some contexts, it is not appropriate for engineering sales. First, the engineer is a professional who offers his special expertise as a professional. Engineering sales usually involve fairly technical matters and cannot proceed if the buyer does not place considerable trust in the seller. In these respects engineering sales differ from selling a used car. When I purchase a used car, the saleswoman does not present herself as an expert, and I am in a position to have the car thoroughly checked out by my own mechanic before buying it. I am in as good a position to assess the car as is the saleswoman and in a better position to gauge my own needs than she is. So I do not need a used car salesperson to act as a consultant. In engineering sales, however, the buyer is usually not in a good position to evaluate the product on his own and must rely upon the salesperson's representations to a significant extent. Moreover, the buyer is not necessarily well situated to determine which product best suits his needs. Thus, most buyers need the engineering salesperson to act as a consultant. And so, if a buyer has a reasonable choice between purchasing from an adversarial and a consulting salesperson, the buyer will almost always purchase from the consulting salesperson. Customers would rather buy from a trustworthy advisor than from a "snake oil" salesperson. Buyers prefer companies they can trust, and a salesperson who misrepresents a product or sells a buyer a product that does not suit the buyer's needs does his company long-term harm.

Second, from the ethical standpoint, consulting sales promote the best consequences, since everyone benefits: consulting sales best suit the customer's needs and produce more sales for the salesperson's company. In addition, clean, clear decision making is a value of the engineering profession. Clean, clear decision making is not possible without the relevant facts, so if the salesperson hid relevant facts, that would be an attempt to undermine a value of the engineering profession. Consulting sales promote this value, while adversarial sales undermine it.

Finally, adversarial sales are less likely than consulting sales to advance human welfare. Human progress is not best served by customers using inappropriate products out of ignorance. Thus, ethics and business sense both dictate that the engineering salesperson establish a consulting sales relationship rather than an adversarial one.

Anyone who presents himself as a consulting salesperson, inviting the buyer to rely upon him, has a moral obligation to live up to that promise. The value of honesty, the principle of universality, and the rules for treating others fairly all forbid the salesperson from obtaining a sale by posing as a consulting salesperson and then abusing that trust by steering the customer wrong. Indeed, someone who represents himself as a consulting salesperson has an institutional duty to do his best to meet the customer's needs, since he is able to function as a consulting salesperson only because customers rely upon his faithfully performing the duties of a consulting salesperson.

We can summarize these points with the following specific rule: be a (faithful) consulting salesperson rather than an adversarial salesperson.

Illustrating Case

Case 33: While discussing her product with a customer, a sales engineer realizes that a competitor's product serves her customer's needs better than her own does: although her product does have one or two advantages, it costs significantly more than the competitor's product because it has features that the customer does not need for his application. How should the sales engineer handle the situation?

Discussion: Most writers argue that the company's long-term interest is best served by honesty. ''If the sales engineer sells a customer a product [that] is not as satisfactory for a particular application as a competitor's product would be, the customer may very well discover the fact and thereafter be suspicious of the company [that] sold him the product, or even stop all business relations with it.''[16]

The rule that one should be a faithful consulting salesperson requires that the sales engineer be honest. However, since the customer makes the ultimate decision, the sales engineer should not be shy about urging whatever legitimate advantages her product can offer, even if, in her judgment, the competitor's product better suits the customer's needs overall. In short, the sales engineer should be frank about the drawbacks of her product relative to a competitor's, should emphasize whatever legitimate advantages her product can offer, and should leave the ultimate decision to the customer.

6

Good Faith

The following set of issues deal with acting in good faith, both in fact and appearance. Engineers often find themselves in situations where others must rely upon their integrity. In bidding, keeping information confidential, respecting patents and copyrights, and potential conflict of interest situations, the engineer is expected to refrain from compromising the trust placed in her; her personal motivations must take second place to the integrity of the process.

Conflict of Interest

Conflicts of interest are situations in which other interests place a strain upon the loyalty of an engineer to do the very best he can for his company (or, in the case of a consulting engineer, for his client). Conflicts of interest are, to a certain extent, inevitable. The ethical engineer may experience a conflict between the firm's or company's interests and moral imperatives such as protecting public safety or respecting nature. If a neighbor or cousin of a procurement engineer works for a supplier, that engineer has a motivation to favor (or avoid) that supplier, and this motivation may affect the engineer's judgment. Conflict of interest situations thus have two ethical aspects. First, to the extent feasible, avoid situations that might bias, or appear to others to bias, one's judgment on the firm's or company's behalf. Second, when avoidance is impossible, observe strict impartiality, both in appearance and in fact.

Some conflict of interest situations are obvious, while others are less obvious. Conflicts of interest may arise when one engages in activities that compete with the company. This would include owning stock in competing firms or companies and marketing a product that competes with the company's product. Thus, an engineer who works for a company with extensive oil or mining interests should not speculate in oil and mineral rights. Conflicts may also arise when employees have relationships with suppliers that may compromise their judgment. Thus, engineers should avoid accepting gifts with more than nominal value (often set at twenty-five dollars), accepting extravagant entertainment or special discounts not available to other members of the company, receiving cash payments or loans, moonlighting for suppliers, conducting noncompany business transactions with suppliers, and owning stock in supplier companies. Potential conflicts result when an engineer conducts business with his company, such as by selling real estate to the company, leasing equipment to the company, and selling engineering, contracting, managerial, or financial services to the company. Ethical conduct in company employment relations with relatives, another conflict of interest situation, includes avoiding determining the salary, raises, promotions, or bonuses of close family members. Finally, conflict of interest results when one uses for personal gain one's position in the firm or company, company facilities, or knowledge of the firm's or company's affairs. Examples include speculating on real estate using inside knowledge of company plans and using company equipment or supplies for personal uses.[1]

Robert E. Frederick suggests that firms and companies create a statement of company policy that details procedures for clear-cut cases and establish a mechanism (such as a committee) for dealing with borderline cases, which employees must consult in new or questionable cases.[2] In addition, the company must make new policies known to employees and impose penalties for violating the policy.

Confidentiality and Trade Secrets

Companies need to maintain discretion to protect five kinds of information: the privacy of individuals (for example, do not reveal the age or health of an employee), the integrity of decision processes (for instance, do not reveal the contents of a confidential letter of recommendation for an employee), trade secrets (do not reveal unpatented secret processes, formulae, etc.), business plans (for example, do not leak insider information that might affect the stock market or reveal the location of a projected plant that might affect real estate prices), and client information, including information whose secrecy is desired by your company (do not reveal lists of clients and suppliers) and information whose secrecy is desired by the client (do not disclose client's trade secrets or business plans). None of these rules is absolute, and they are often difficult to apply. The remarks below are intended to help in their application. (See also "When to Break the Rules" in Chapter 4.)

In thinking about protecting the confidentiality of the decision process, remember that the point of the practice of confidentiality here is to enable people to speak candidly without fear of reprisal or embarrassment, to protect honest decision making, not evildoing. Intelligent decision making requires candor, not evil, slander, and unfairness. Thus, you generally must keep confidential the contents of a confidential letter of reference. The honest judgment of a letter writer must be respected, even if one disagrees. However, if the letter unfairly slanders the employee or contains patently false information, you may consider it necessary to inform the writer of the letter of this fact, discuss the matter, and in the worst case, threaten to tell the employee if the writer does not change his letter. Needless to say, engineers must respect all legal duties regarding confidentiality of letters of reference.

Perhaps the most problematic case concerns engineers who leave one employer for another. Clearly, while an engineer may use the general knowledge she has acquired over the years, she should regard the trade secrets of her previous employer as confidential. In practice, however, the distinction is not an easy one to draw. Philip Alger and coauthors mention several relevant factors: "1) the extent to which the information is known outside the business; 2) the extent to which it is known by employees and others involved in [the] business; 3) the extent of measures taken to guard the secrecy of the information; 4) the value of the information to holders and to competitors; 5) the amount of effort or money expended in developing the information;

[and] 6) the ease or difficulty with which the information could be properly acquired or duplicated by others."[3] These factors are not always easy to assess.

Moreover, as Mike Martin and Roland Schinzinger put it, "[A]n engineer's knowledge-base generates an intuitive sense of what designs will or will not work, and trade secrets form part of this knowledge base."[4] However scrupulous an employee is, he cannot help drawing upon the fruits of his past experience. For example, no one would expect an engineer to repeat the effort of trying out a design he already knows, from past experience at another company, will fail. Thus, engineers have to draw upon past employers' trade secrets, at least to the extent of knowing what not to try.

This suggests several points about confidentiality. First, engineers should make every effort to avoid changing companies, when feasible. They should try to work things out with their present employer rather than change jobs. Engineers should not accept employment if they believe the motive for the offer is their knowledge of trade secrets. Second, engineers should not explicitly reveal trade secrets and must be skittish about drawing upon special knowledge paid for by their previous employer. Nevertheless, employment is a kind of partnership, and the general knowledge, skill, and experience an employee gains in her job is part of her remuneration. Third, since innovation is a key engineering value, engineers should seek new approaches to problems they have worked on under a previous employer rather than seek to duplicate or make minor variations to secret processes. Taking a thoroughly new approach minimizes the danger of using the trade secrets of a past employer and maximizes the possibility of advancing human knowledge and welfare. Honesty and communication can often avert or resolve problems.

Employers can also take steps to minimize problems. Michael Baram suggests several measures, including ''prohibition of consulting and other 'moonlighting,' dissemination of trade secrets on a strict 'need to know' basis to designated employees, . . . prohibitions on the copying of trade secret data . . . restrict research and other operational areas to access for designated 'badge' employees only and divide up operations to prevent the accumulation of extensive knowledge by any individual . . . distribute unmarked materials—particularly chemicals—to employees.'' Baram notes, however, that these policies ''must be exercised with a sophisticated regard for employee motivation . . . because the cumulative effect may result in a police state atmosphere that inhibits creativity and repels prospective employees.''[5] Baram also suggests that employers provide incentives for departing employees to opt not to work for a competitor. For example, such employees might retain their pension funds or be eligible for an annual consulting fee if they do not work for a competitor. Finally, Baram recommends debriefing departing employees.

Illustrating Case

Case 34: Migenes' old employer, Division Drugs, developed an adaptation of standard equipment that makes it more efficient at holding drugs at a standard temperature during their manufacture.[6] The adaptation is a trade secret. Migenes goes to work for a petrochemical company,

Mardon, not in competition with Division Drugs. She realizes that a similar adaptation might be made to a different machine to make a very efficient temperature controller in the production of a synthetic rubber.

Discussion: This case walks the line between general experience and trade secrets—although the process is similar, the engineer applies it to a different machine for a different purpose, which requires some imagination and insight on her part. Here the importance of honesty and communication becomes evident. Migenes should contact Division Drugs and ask permission to make the change, after informing Mardon that she will do so.

Patents and Copyrights

It is certainly unethical to violate patent and copyright laws. However, by making a few minor modifications to the patented or copyrighted item, an engineer often may legally duplicate what is basically a patented or copyrighted product or process. Is it unethical to make a minor modification in a patented process or product (or copyrighted program) to avoid copyright infringement?

The patent and copyright laws are a compromise between two competing aims. On the one hand, creators and innovators deserve to enjoy the fruits of their labor. To deprive them of the benefits of their innovation would be unjust (a kind of theft) and socially harmful: without patents, the incentive to innovate would be lessened, resulting in fewer innovations, and innovators would have to rely on secrecy, thus undermining the communication and cooperation necessary for progress. Thus, the principles of promoting justice (treating others fairly and well), human welfare, and good consequences require that ethical engineers not infringe on patents and copyrights. Nonetheless, society has an interest in the development and improvement of innovations and in the widespread use of beneficial technologies. (That is why patents are granted for a fixed term rather than forever.) In other words, the ethics of copyrights and patents tries to balance being fair to the innovator with spreading and improving technology to advance human welfare.

This attempt at balance suggests some factors engineers may weigh. First, has the innovator had a chance to benefit from the innovation? Some patents yield profits immediately, while others take a long time to pay back investment costs. It is less troubling to market a modified patented product if the innovator has had a reasonable chance to profit from the innovation. Second, is the modification a real improvement, or was it developed only to get around the patent laws? It is less troubling to market a modified product that truly advances human welfare. If the modification makes the product safer, more precise, more useful, more widely available (either by being cheaper or by fitting current procedures or machinery), or less environmentally harmful, marketing the modified product is generally justifiable. Third, how significant a change is the modification? Changing a few unimportant lines in a program is more troubling than making major alterations in machinery. Finally, is there any doubt about the legality of marketing the modification? Engineers should never engage in legally questionable practices.

Bidding

The engineering profession cannot operate as it does without public recognition of trust: reliance in the strict probity and fairness of bidding and supplying procedures is a precondition for engineers to function as they do. Hence, engineers have an institutional duty to observe strict propriety in these matters. The rules of propriety in bidding are central to the practice of engineering. Moreover, since the firms involved in supplying and bidding on contracts are competitors, the situation is conflictful. Finally, trust is an essential factor, and so the appearance of impropriety is almost as damaging as actual impropriety. The legitimate gain in bending these rules is minor. Thus, there is a very strong case for strict adherence to rules of propriety. In general, engineers should err in the direction of caution in giving or accepting anything that smacks of a favor or gift, in acquiring an interest in a supplier or potential contractor, and so forth. The rule of thumb is "If there's any doubt, don't do it."

To help you in thinking about this, William Shaw and Vincent Barry list seven questions you should ask yourself about a gift.[7]

1. What is the value of the gift?
2. What is the purpose of the gift?
3. What are the circumstances under which the gift was given or received?
4. What is the position and sensitivity to influence of the person receiving the gift?
5. What is the accepted business practice in the area?
6. What is the company's policy?
7. What is the law?

Most larger companies and firms have corporate policy statements on gifts. For example, Honeywell's statement asserts that "acceptance or giving of gifts must be limited to incidentals [that] are obviously a custom of the trade, are acceptable as items of insignificant value, or in no way would cause the Company [or firm] to be embarrassed or obligated. . . . If return of a gift is not practicable because of its nature, it may be given to a charitable institution and the supplier [should be] informed of its disposition."[8]

Illustrating Cases

Case 35: After many years of experience, you come to believe that Y is the best supplier. May you cease taking competitive bids, and is it ethical to take bids when the decision has already been made? How should the situation be handled? What are the governing considerations? (See the discussion of Case 22 in Chapter 4.)

Case 36: You are genuinely interested in the equipment of firm Y. Y offers to pay expenses for you to visit a plant in which Y's equipment is used or the plant at which the equipment is produced. Is it ethical to accept? (Note: Alger says about a similar case that "if there is no other possible way for the engineer to get the necessary information . . . he should make the trip, with the understanding that, in accepting this invitation, he is incurring no obligation to the company."[9])

Case 37: You are a purchasing agent responsible for ordering trucks and other automotive equipment. For several years you have purchased reliable and inexpensive trucks from a particular dealer. This dealer also sells recreational vehicles. When you go to the dealer to purchase a recreational vehicle for your own use, the dealer offers to sell you the vehicle at a price well below what it generally sells for.

Discussion: Clearly, the dealer is offering you a personal discount with the intention of influencing your judgment. He is not offering the discount to the firm (which would be a legitimate sales incentive) but to you personally. His purpose is not to persuade you to buy more vehicles for yourself but to ensure that you continue to place orders with him for the firm. A substantial amount of money is involved, and the discount is not available to the general public. You cannot deny that the dealer is offering you a bribe. True, the dealer did not explicitly say "I expect you to continue to purchase your company's vehicles from me," but his intention in offering the discount is clear. Thus, accepting the discount is unethical. After all, if you accept the discount, you make an unspoken promise: you create an obligation to the dealer that violates your duty as a purchasing agent for your company. Suppose, for example, that next month another supplier offers a better deal to your company. If you do not switch suppliers, you betray your company. If you do switch companies, you break a tacit promise to the dealer (at the very least, you treat him unfairly and take advantage of him). Accepting the discount creates psychological pressure on you to continue buying from this dealer: it motivates you to regard his offer in the best possible light, to look for flaws in other suppliers, and so forth. Even were you to say explicitly to the dealer when accepting the discount that your judgment on behalf of your company will not be influenced, you will find it difficult in future to be completely unbiased. In any case, accepting the discount creates the appearance of impropriety, and in bidding the appearance of impropriety should be avoided if at all possible. The Golden Rule helps resolve this case: how would you feel if you were bidding to supply the Z company and discovered that the purchasing agent for the Z company had accepted a large personal discount from one of your competitors?

Case 38: You are taking sales proposals for a particular piece of equipment. Is it ethical for you to discuss the features of one vendor's equipment with another supplier?

Discussion: "While no supplier can hope to keep a special feature or design for his exclusive use for long, he is entitled to full protection on any special design or feature he offers on any specific purchase."[10] However, on products offered in the open market, protection of special features must come from copyrights, and buyers are entitled to hear how one vendor would answer the claims of another. This problem is to be contrasted with the next.

Case 39: You are taking proposals for a complex project. Is it ethical for you to take one of the ideas in bidder N's proposal and adopt it as your own by revising the specifications and then asking the other bidders for revised bids?

Discussion: To the extent that the idea taken from bidder N's proposal is innovative or results from special expertise, taking the idea without paying for it is stealing. The ethical thing to do, generally, is to evaluate N's overall proposal, including this idea, against the other proposals as they stand. If bidder Q's overall proposal is the best, you may, after making it clear that you have accepted bidder Q's proposal, ask N for permission to use that idea. (Special circumstances may call for special arrangements. For example, if N's idea is crucial but N's proposal is for some other reason truly unacceptable, some sort of special arrangement seems called for. In some cases, it may be feasible to ask N and Q to collaborate.) A more thorough design study prior to asking for bids might have eliminated the problem.

Case 40: Is it ethical to own stock in the Chemical Equipment Corporation (CEC)? Consider the following possibilities:

1. You already own stock in CEC, a company with which you personally have had no dealings. However, you are assigned to a new project and as part of your new duties must take bids on a type of item that CEC, among others, manufactures.
2. Your duties include, from time to time, taking bids on various sorts of chemical equipment. Your stockbroker suggests to you that CEC would be an excellent investment. (Does it matter whether you personally have, or whether your company has, ever received a bid from CEC?)
3. CEC is a competing company.
4. Your duties include working with several officers of CEC. As a result of this collaboration, you become aware of several features of CEC that suggest to you that CEC will grow significantly over the next several years.

Is it ethical in any of these situations to purchase or retain existing stock in CEC?

Discussion: Owning stock in a chemical equipment company, when your duties even tangentially involve assessing bids from such companies, creates the appearance of impropriety and may in fact create a conflict between your personal interest and exercising your best judgment on your company's behalf. For these reasons you should avoid owning stock in CEC. Of course, not all such conflicts can be avoided: it would be absurd to insist that you may not become a chemical engineer if your older cousin already works for a chemical equipment company. Some situations in which you may face psychological pressure to make biased choices are inevitable. Nonetheless, one should avoid those situations whenever possible, and it is generally a simple matter not to purchase stocks in companies that supply items of a sort your company bids upon. Even if you have never received a bid from CEC, the possibility of conflict of interest exists. (You or your company may receive bids from CEC in the future, and you may be more inclined to find fault with other company's products. In fact, if you buy CEC stock, ethical considerations may inhibit you from investigating as thoroughly as you otherwise might what CEC can do for your company.) If you already have a significant holding in such a company, you should sell. (Many companies do permit engineers to own stock in supplier companies, as long as the stock owned constitutes less than a certain percentage of the total stock of the company.) In addition, buying stock on the basis of certain kinds of insider information is illegal, and even when not specifically prohibited by law, it is bad practice to use your position within the company for personal advantage in the stock market. Finally, buying stock in a competing company not only gives one a financial incentive to do less than one's best for one's own company, but also undercuts loyalty and community spirit, and so is a bad idea.

Case 41: Is it ethical for corporate officers to have their cars repaired or serviced by the company's repair shop or to have repair work on their homes done by company workers on company time? Is it ethical for an executive to have her secretary run personal errands for her? Is it ethical to ask idle workers to do repairs on one's home? Is it ethical to ask subordinates to hang decorations in one's home for an upcoming company party?

Discussion: A line must be drawn between fringe benefits and abusing one's position. If you ask company employees to do things for you on company time to which you are not entitled, you are stealing. The company, after all, is paying for the employee's time, and you are taking that time for your own personal use. If you take an hour of a secretary's company-paid time to buy a birthday present for your daughter, that is no different from simply taking the amount of the secretary's hourly wage from the cash drawer. Even if the secretary would otherwise be idle, you are taking for your own use the money the company pays for that hour. Making illicit personal use of company personnel is just another form of embezzling from the company. By contrast, the use of a company car can be a legitimate fringe benefit. Questions to ask oneself include the following: What are the rules of the company? Is it lawful? Is this an explicit fringe benefit, and how is it carried on the company's books? What is the accepted business practice? How would it look if it were made public? Is a legitimate business function involved (for example, is your house used for company meetings)? Finally, it goes without saying that putting pressure on employees to do personal errands or favors on their own time is highly improper and unethical.

Case 42: Is it ethical for a corporate engineer to "rescue" something from a company garbage can or dump site to be used for private purposes?

Discussion: It may be tempting to regard the item in the dump site as abandoned property and so decide that taking it would not be stealing. However, if the item discarded is still usable, loyalty to the company suggests that one has a duty to call the matter to the company's attention. In any case, the ethical thing to do is clear: ask permission before taking the item. Simply taking the item is, at best, not being straightforward and may violate company policy.

Case 43: Is it ethical for engineers to make copies of software purchased by the company for (1) their own enjoyment or family use (such as a diagnostic program used in a recreational project or a word processing program used by a son or daughter in school), (2) use in helping friends or civic groups, or (3) profitable projects?

Case 44: Is it ethical for an engineer to take home a pencil for use on company business to be done at home? Is it always easy to distinguish between company and personal use? (Consider the situation of someone with vision problems who uses a magnifying glass when reading professional periodicals and someone taking a "refresher" engineering course at night. These are not strictly company activities, but they do benefit the company by helping to make one a better engineer.)

Case 45: You are invited by the Left-Handed Engineers of America to give a paper to the LHEA on your recent work in the manufacture of synthetic leather.

Discussion: The values of advancing human knowledge and collegiality within the engineering community mean that participation in professional meetings is an important aspect of professional life. However, duties of confidentiality mean that one should not disclose secrets whose dissemination would hurt the company. The way to resolve this conflict is to clear your presentation with your company. Since few companies could operate without considerable cooperation in sharing information, the principle of universality suggests that companies must do their part in advancing the general knowledge shared by engineering as a field. Thus, cooperation is worth a minor risk of inconvenience or loss of competitive advantage to the company, though of course no company ought to part with information that would hurt it significantly. It follows that your company should strive to assist you in sharing as much information as feasible, short of significantly hurting the company.[11]

7

Employee-Employer Relations

Engineers rarely work alone; engineering operations generally require a team of engineers, support personnel, and business expertise (management, accounting, and
sales). Thus, virtually all engineers are employed or
employ others, and virtually all engineers have superiors or
subordinates. As an engineer, you must make employment
decisions. This chapter will help you make those decisions
fairly and ethically.

Types of Work Relationships

Bruce F. Gordon and Ian C. Ross identify three kinds of
work relationships. In an artisan-master relationship, the
employee does what the employer wants. In a professional
status relationship, the employee gives the employer what
the employer ought to have. Finally, in a protégé-patron
relationship, the employee gives the employer what the
employee wants (for example, researchers who determine
their own research programs).[1] Gordon and Ross suggest
that a modern research organization may employ different

192

individuals in all three categories. I would suggest, instead, that all engineers belong, to a greater or lesser extent, in all three categories. All engineers are bound by company rules and policies and must be guided, to some extent, by the company's needs. In this sense all engineers are "artisans." But engineers also have a duty to use their brains, to be innovative, and to speak up on the company's behalf, and most companies welcome suggestions from engineers. Indeed, because engineers must take some responsibility for what goes on in the company, they have a duty not to follow orders mindlessly, without thinking about what ought to happen (see "Principles of Accountability" in Chapter 4). In this sense, all engineers have "professional status." Finally, every engineer is an artist engaged in the great social task of advancing human welfare and so, within the limits set for him, should be giving the employer what he, the engineer, wants to give, namely, his best ideas and effort. In this sense, the engineer is an artist sponsored by the company in a "protégé-patron relationship."

Balancing these three elements of the work relationship is not always easy. You might want to ask yourself the following questions when trying to strike a proper balance.

First, what is the nature of the work I am asked to do? Some tasks leave more room for freedom than others. For example, an engineer in a research and development department with the primary idea for a new product has more room for "artistic freedom" than does an engineer writing specifications for a cooling system.

Second, what is at stake if I give my firm or company what it ought to have instead of what it asks of me? For example, an engineer responsible for the safety of a nuclear reactor has a duty to give the employer what the employer ought to have, rather than what the employer wants, since an unsafe nuclear reactor creates an unacceptable risk to the public. By contrast, while a manufacturing engineer who sees a more efficient way to do what he is asked to do should certainly point out his idea to his supervisor, if the supervisor insists it should be done another way, the manufacturing engineer should do what the supervisor wants, since what is at stake here is not the public's safety but the employer's money. In the case of consulting engineering, it is ultimately the firm rather than the individual engineer who is responsible for seeing to the best interests of the client, and it is ultimately the client rather than the firm who is responsible for the successful use of the project. Thus, when safety and ethics are not involved, the firm must ultimately give way to the client, and the individual engineer employed by a consulting firm must ultimately give way to the firm.

Third, what particular understanding do I have with my company or firm? A company may give some researchers a freer hand than others, and some companies are less comfortable with "giving researchers their head" than others.

In all three kinds of employment relations, fair treatment and a community atmosphere are crucial for employee motivation. Supervisors and employers can do much to help generate this kind of work environment.

Leadership and Healthy Work Environments

Books on leadership and management fill shelf after shelf in libraries and bookstores. Within these books you will find many theories of good management. Two views of supervision deserve special mention. Supervisors often view themselves as lords of the castle: their role, as they see it, is to give orders, make decisions, and see to it that their subordinates obey. Other supervisors see themselves as facilitators more than order-givers: their role is to help their subordinates function efficiently and cooperatively. In general, facilitators make better supervisors than order-givers do, since a facilitator permits subordinates to feel that they are valuable and productive members of a team, doing their best to contribute in the way they best understand. Facilitators help create a community atmosphere and show respect for persons. As a result, subordinates do better work and feel more job satisfaction and company loyalty. Order-givers, who hand down decisions, may lack the experience and perception of subordinates who actually do the work. While many U.S. companies attempt to emulate Japanese methods of involving subordinates in company decisions (such as "total quality management"), their attempts are doomed to fail if supervisors still perceive themselves as lords of the castle. A supervisor who tells a subordinate "Get your butt in my office" cannot expect the same subordinate, an hour later, to participate in a meeting as a valued member of the team. To be a good facilitator, a supervisor must bring the appropriate frame of mind to everything she does. An order-giver shows authority by barking commands and making threats. A facilitator's authority shows in her dedication, her self-assurance, her clearness of purpose, her fairness, her ability to make tough decisions when necessary, and her competence, knowledge, and perception (the sense that one cannot "put one over" on her). Establishing a working team environment within a department takes hard work, skill, and care. The results justify the effort.

Facilitators and order-givers use different motivational strategies. Facilitators use incentives that promote teamwork and ethical behavior. For example, a manager who offers a bonus to the individual with the most sales in her department turns that department's sales staff into competitors; each salesperson has a strong reason to hope that his colleagues fail. How can a manager expect one salesperson to assist another when doing so threatens his bonus? Facilitators, who try to promote teamwork, are creative in providing incentives that promote cooperation instead of competition. Similarly, offering captains of oil tankers a bonus for arriving early gives them an incentive to cut corners, cheat on safety drills, and so forth. Facilitators, who wish to promote ethical conduct, avoid incentives that reward unsafe or unethical conduct. Evaluating subordinates on the basis of bottom-line figures pressures subordinates to enhance their figures by taking shortcuts, taking improper risks, and favoring short-term goals over long-term goals. (A department head has little reason to invest in research and development, for example, when there may be no payoff for five years: by that time, the department head will probably have moved on, and someone else will get the credit.) Facilitators, who want a team dedicated to the company's long-term interests, will evaluate subordinates on the basis of their long-term contribution to the company. Since fear is a powerful short-term motivator, order-givers often try to motivate subordinates through fear. Since fear is a poor long-term motivator, facilitators use fear only as a last resort.

Good facilitators concentrate on two key features of supervision: communication and leadership. It is harder to establish good communication than one might think. R. P. Cort found that, in 100 businesses studied, workers could not understand 80 percent of the information sent down from top management.[2] James Humber points out several reasons for lack of communication:

top management tends to isolate itself to avoid interruption and
   confrontation;
subordinates are reluctant to pass up unfavorable information;
   superiors avoid passing on unfavorable information because
   they do not wish to lower morale; and
in large firms and companies, top and local management rarely
   meet, and it is often difficult to determine who should receive
   the information.[3]

Leadership is, in many ways, the key to a good work environment. According to Tom Peters and Nancy Austin, "leadership means vision, cheerleading, enthusiasm, love, trust, verve, passion, obsession, consistency, the use of symbols, paying attention as illustrated by the content of one's calendar, out-and-out drama . . . creating heroes at all levels, coaching, effectively wandering around, and numerous other things."[4] They recommend what they call "naive listening," that is, sending everyone in the company (including executives, people in research and development, and hourly wage earners) to vendors and customers, and bringing vendors and customers to the company, so that the customer and vendor come alive for employees and executives (and vice versa). The key point is listening to what is actually being said rather than hearing what one expects to hear. For example, Peters and Austin note, Apple has its entire executive staff regularly listen in on the customer call-in 800 number; a Levi Strauss executive spent a weekend selling blue jeans; Campbell's Soup regularly sends executives to the kitchens of three hundred families; Milliken and Company invites customers to visit the specific factory at which their product is made and forms joint problem-solving teams with customers that include hourly wage earners from both sides; People's Express puts letters from customers (including complaints) in a centralized bulletin board; 3M requires its people in research and development to make regular sales calls; and every Tandem facility has a weekly "beer bust" to which all employees are invited.[5] Peters and Austin note the following advantages to these techniques: "Many say that more business is done in those couple of hours than during the rest of the week combined"; "At Hewlett-Packard, each engineer leaves the project he or she is working with out 'on the bench.' Other engineers . . . take a look at it, play with it, comment on it."[6] Peters and Austin suggest that "if you're an R&D VP, make sure you have a second (non-headquarters) office in a lab."[7]

Peters and Austin point out that these techniques foster innovation, since many ideas come from customers or those who deal directly with products or processes, such as linemen. I want to point out that these techniques also help foster a sense of community. Without that sense of community, engineers cannot feel satisfaction from being part of a well-functioning team.

Srully Blotnick points out what happens to the person who takes little or no satisfaction from being part of a team doing a good job.[8] Such a person tends to think about beating the system and shows an inability to accept authority. He needs more and more money, since work fails to satisfy him, but does less and less to earn it. The effects of this pattern are bitterness, goofing off, and dishonesty. He may feel an excessive need to stand out, feeling that teamwork will make him anonymous, and he will have no credentials to take with him if he needs a new job. As some of the people in Blotnick's book say, "Just doing my job isn't getting me the notice I need," and "You have to make people see what you personally can do."[9] Unfortunately, once one person starts hogging credit, he or she forces everyone else to be "me-oriented" in self-defense. By contrast, Blotnick points out, the best kind of teamwork arises when each person is "busy, day after day, doing what he or she does best."[10]

Blotnick mentions two further harmful patterns: anxiety about becoming obsolete and deliberate amnesia of past accomplishments. Anxiety about becoming obsolete often indicates that something else is wrong, that the employee has gotten off the right track. Sometimes this anxiety arises because the person does not recognize that she now has the authority to institute projects and changes or because she does not realize that praise is sparser in a higher-level position, since superiors think it is less needed. Thus, the diminishing of praise is just a normal sign of advancement. Someone afraid of becoming obsolete feels the fear of pressure from below, engages in lobbying efforts to prove she is needed, sandbags subordinates, and tends to be indecisive.

The second pattern is a strategy for motivating oneself. Some people make a practice of forgetting their past accomplishments. But Blotnick contends that you should savor victory when you get it, then move on. (It loses its flavor if you wait until the next project has started.) If you downgrade your past accomplishments, you will have nothing to take with you into the later part of your career. What counts as an ''achievement'' keeps escalating. This may lead to resenting subordinates or getting involved in overly ambitious undertakings (lacking a sense of reality). The pressure to achieve more and more may actually make you less productive.

Protégés

Blotnick also has some insightful remarks about conducting a protégé relationship. Protégé-mentor relationships may go sour for several reasons. Executives are often fearful of giving away anything important, then complain because the protégé does not listen. Too often the mentor spends a great deal of time sharing complaints about the company. This does not help the protégé. After all, if you want people to listen to you, you must give them something worth listening to. Again, executives sometimes look for someone who will humor them instead of a serious protégé who wants to learn. In general, says Blotnick, the people you take under your wing should not be more than twenty years younger than you are, or the disparity between your concerns and perceptions will be too great. Keep a loose and flexible relationship and realize that your protégé will have her own way of doing things. Finally, if the relationship feels like a drain or a chore, this is a strong signal that something has gone wrong. A mentor-protégé relationship should be a two-way street.

Dealing with Subordinates

Allan Firmage makes several useful points about dealing with one's subordinates. Supervisors tend to assign repetitive work to the same employee, thinking he or she will learn to perform it better and quicker. This may work for a while, but boredom quickly sets in.[11] Recognition awards "should not be a substitute for a simple 'well done.'" In the case of inadequate performance, the supervisor should inform the employee constructively, with a program of improvement formulated in a "joint conference" between supervisor and employee. Firms should "encourage and reward" membership in and attendance at meetings of technical societies. This may involve paying part of the membership dues, allowing reasonable time off to attend meetings, and encouraging the presenting and publishing of papers. Employers should maintain a neat and attractive office environment. Self-esteem is advanced when each employee has his or her own work area with proper furnishings.[12]

To these suggestions may be added W. H. Roadstrum's more general reminder that "a good rule in dealing with others is to work from the highest common purposes possible while not overlooking the economic motive."[13] Moreover, says Roadstrum, an employee's need for a good self-image is often as important as his economic needs. Employers should avoid "threats against self-image" when feasible, as employees' fulfillment needs are often as important as the economic needs.[14]

In addition to these suggestions, employers should generally follow certain rules of ethical behavior: "No public or private organization shall discriminate against an employee for criticizing the ethical, moral or legal policies and practices of the organization; nor shall any organization discriminate against an employee for engaging in outside activities of his or her choice [that do not violate the engineer's duties as an engineer or an employee], or for objecting to a directive that violates common norms of morality."[15] (I added the words in brackets because some outside activities, such as moonlighting for a competitor, might be licit grounds for employer sanctions.) Further, "no organization shall deprive an employee of the enjoyment of reasonable privacy in his or her place of work, and no personal information about employees shall be collected or kept other than that necessary to manage the organization efficiently and to meet legal requirements. . . . No employee of a public or private organization who alleges in good faith that his or her rights have been violated shall be discharged or penalized without a fair hearing in the employer organization. . . . In a personal interview, the employer should inform the employee of the specific reasons for his/her termination."[16]

Friendship, Favoritism, and Professional Relations

Friendship in the workplace is both a valuable component of a healthy work environment and an ethically sensitive issue. (Note that this section discusses *friendship* in the workplace, not sex. The term *fraternization* comes from a Latin word meaning "brotherhood.") Supervisors have an obligation to protect subordinates from personal pressures, both explicit and subtle. They can fulfill this duty in one of two ways. In the first, rigid nonfraternization rules mandate that supervisors should never socialize with subordinates, physicians should never socialize with patients, and faculty should never socialize with students. In the second, supervisors reestablish the ideal of integrity in work decisions.

These two methods, the ideal of integrity and the rule of nonfraternization, lead to very different kinds of work communities. The rule of nonfraternization insists that you have no personal dealings with subordinates. The ideal of integrity insists that your personal feelings for or against subordinates must not influence your professional decisions. For example, the rule of nonfraternization says you should avoid taking nonworking lunches with subordinates. The ideal of integrity permits and even encourages social lunches but dictates that your subordinates must have absolute confidence that, when you award promotions, you do so entirely on the basis of job-related merit; that those who join you for lunch will not, on that account, be favored; and that those who do not join you for lunch will not, on that account, be penalized.

The ethical engineer will, of course, observe the limits of social behavior between supervisor and subordinate that the law requires and will not violate company policy. I do suggest that to the extent that the engineer has some latitude, he or she should generally favor the ideal of integrity over rigid nonfraternization rules.

Nonfraternization rules have several harmful effects.

Most immediately, they produce a class-dominated society. If we make it taboo for a manager to talk about her personal problems with her assistant, we send a strong message to the assistant: you are not the social equal of your boss; you are unclean; you are not a subordinate merely in terms of work responsibility but in your personal life as well. And we send a message to the executive: your assistant is not a person but another business machine. As a result, work relations become purely instrumental. Employees become not a community of mutually concerned persons with common goals and values but a well-oiled business machine. Fellow employees become not teammates who care about each other but impersonal cogs and wheels. Thus, nonfraternization rules establish an atmosphere of impersonal efficiency rather than an atmosphere of fellowship based on pursuing a common goal. This further alienates people from their work.

In many fields, nonfraternization rules lower the quality of work. Impersonalization leads to bad engineering because the element of comradeship and joint innovation disappears. Impersonalization leads to bad medicine because physicians tend to view patients simply as raw material for their skills, not as persons with unique goals and concerns. They are prompted to view their work not as a calling to which they bring the whole of their humanity but as an impersonal technical exercise. Impersonalization leads to bad education because faculty members view students not as members of a community in whose development as thinking human beings they have a personal concern but as data banks to be filled with information or programs (skills).

Finally, nonfraternization rules lead, ironically enough, to a lack of ethics in the work world, since efficiency replaces humanity and propriety replaces values. When rules replace integrity, what becomes important is not the values associated with integrity but simply keeping to the rules. The ethical dimension drops out, leaving only a game with arbitrary rules to be manipulated to one's advantage.

What should govern most work relations is the ideal of integrity. Integrity calls for special efforts from everyone involved, because it involves trust, and trust must be built and nurtured. It is much easier to keep to a set of rules than it is to use good judgment and build trust, but both human decency and good business practice require the extra effort.

You can build integrity into your employment and managerial decisions in several ways. First, let your actions speak for you: if your decisions are unfair, nothing will disguise that fact for very long. Second, make sure that when your subordinates cannot get what they wish, they understand the reasons. Open, frank, and cooperative discussion goes a long way toward dispelling suspicion. Subordinates who understand what is going on and learn the reasons for your decisions may not like those decisions, but they are less likely to attribute your decisions to favoritism. Third, fostering a community atmosphere in general helps build trust. Subordinates who compete with one another are always looking over their shoulders and are constantly concerned with whether other employees are getting a better deal. Members of a team are less likely to begrudge each other success.

Of course, in certain circumstances, stringent nonfraternization rules are appropriate, particularly when the appearance of propriety is itself the crucial aim (or one of the most crucial aims) of the activity. In a legal system, for example, assuring the public of the impartiality of judicial proceedings is as important as arriving at just results, for the law's standing depends upon public perception of the law as absolutely impartial. The rule of law is centrally about impartiality: impartiality is the keystone of law, and respect for the authority of law within a society depends upon public perception of impartiality. So there is some sense in a rule that judges should not socialize with practicing attorneys who might come before them. As another example, bidding is a highly competitive practice in which, typically, huge sums of money are involved, and the very process of submitting bids depends critically upon impartiality. Bid taking is centrally about impartiality, and the perception of impartiality is crucial to the practice. Moreover, bid takers and suppliers generally work for different companies; bid takers are not on the same "team" as suppliers, and so the process of building walls between bid takers and suppliers as persons does not compromise the ideal of community. Because suppliers are not subordinate to bid takers, nonfraternization rules do not create a class structure. Thus, building walls between suppliers and bid takers does not dehumanize suppliers. There are good reasons, therefore, for bid takers to adhere to strict rules about accepting from suppliers gifts, meals, and so forth.

By way of contrast, impartiality of grades is not what the university is about: the university is devoted to the cultivation and advancement of wisdom and learning, a goal to which testing and evaluation of students is secondary. Medicine is about healing, about advancing the well-being of people. Building walls between students and faculty or between physicians and patients does undermine the central tasks of education and medicine and does dehumanize patients and students.

The application of these remarks to engineers is fairly clear. Follow faithfully all legal requirements and company policies. Within those limits, follow strict rules of non-fraternization when the context is highly competitive, the perception of impartiality is a central goal of the activity, or building walls between the people involved does not undermine a central task. Otherwise strive for a community atmosphere, taking special care to establish trust in your integrity.

Harassment

Harassment in the workplace takes many forms. Harassment is the creation of an oppressive work environment on the basis of personal characteristics unrelated to job performance, such as gender, race, religion, sexual orientation, weight, height, physical or mental handicaps, and political beliefs, or as retaliation for legitimate job decisions. Harassment is unethical and (in many cases) illegal. It interferes with work and creates serious personal hardship for those who are harassed, for those who witness the harassment, and even, sometimes, for the harasser. The media have given the most attention to sexual harassment, but other forms of harassment are equally serious. Most of the following remarks on sexual harassment apply to other forms of harassment as well.

Sexual harassment, as defined by the Equal Employment Opportunity Commission (EEOC), comes in two forms: quid pro quo and creating an oppressive work environment. In quid pro quo, job advancement or continued employment is made conditional upon giving sexual favors, going out on dates, enduring improper touching, and so forth. Since this kind of harassment constitutes either blackmail or bribery, it is the most ethically serious form of harassment. Quid pro quo severely and immediately violates several ethical considerations, including respect for autonomy, fairness, and the ideal of integrity. Creating an oppressive work environment, while not quite as evil, is nonetheless serious. Individuals deserve a workplace in which they are treated with respect as a valued member of a team and in which they feel personally comfortable. Moreover, sexism is itself an evil, and an ethically aware company will not tolerate it. Many things may contribute to an oppressive work environment, including displaying sexually explicit posters or pictures, touching or sexual joking that would make a reasonable person in our society feel uncomfortable, sexually oriented remarks about a fellow worker's body parts or attire, whistling, looks intended to convey a sexual message (such as leering), trying to peer inside a fellow worker's clothing, and derogatory remarks of a sexual nature.

Sexual harassment is by nature explosive and so must be handled with care and sensitivity. On the one hand, genuine cases of sexual harassment do occur, and harassment has a powerful and degrading effect on the victim. On the other hand, being unjustly accused of sexual harassment is also harmful and upsetting. Both parties, the purported harasser and the purported victim, must be treated fairly and sensitively. One should keep two facts firmly in mind: first, sexual harassment does happen, and second, there is often room for genuine misunderstanding (particularly as many sexual overtures are made indirectly or by the use of euphemisms, and, as a result of cultural and personal differences, what one person regards as a friendly gesture may make another person uncomfortable). The right way to handle sexual harassment, therefore, is cooperatively and openly. Unfortunately, not everyone is ethical. Thus, when the right way fails to work, other steps must be taken.

Someone who feels uncomfortable with what goes on in the workplace should begin by asking himself or herself whether to adjust to the situation or attempt to change it. The answer should depend upon the nature of the discomfort: how uncomfortable does it make you, how reasonable is it for you to feel discomfort, and how easy is it for others to change? For example, if the way a fellow worker touches you makes you feel uncomfortable, you should almost always bring the matter up—it is easy for the other person to refrain from touching you. A male who feels mildly uncomfortable by his female colleagues' discussion of menstruation may decide that his mild discomfort is less important than the bonding these discussions produce. Nevertheless, he should probably mention the problem if he feels significantly uncomfortable, since coworkers can easily refrain from discussing this topic. He has more reason to address the issue if the effect of the discussion is to exclude him.

If you decide to address the issue, you should speak directly to those involved in a friendly and cooperative manner. Do not expect others to read your mind. A hint is not as good as a frank and open discussion. After all, your hints may not be understood. Your scowl or dirty look or veiled comment may be interpreted as a joke or as a reaction to something other than the offending behavior. Moreover, because a hint does not explain where you are coming from, others are more likely to resent you and less likely to do what you ask. It is almost always better, no matter what the problem is, to provide others a face-saving way to give you what you are asking for. For example, if you are uncomfortable because a colleague puts his arm on your shoulder, you might say, ''I realize that you don't mean anything bad by putting your arm on my shoulder, and that it's just a friendly gesture, but it makes me uncomfortable. If you wouldn't mind not doing that, I'd appreciate it.'' Follow it with a small gesture that indicates the request is a friendly one and that you have no hard feelings. Conversely, if someone makes such a request of you, you should assure the person that you take his feelings seriously, that you meant no harm, and that you would be happy to accommodate him. The keys to such interactions are mutual respect, friendliness, cooperation, and a desire to make each other feel better. Keep in mind that in some cultures and in some families friendly touching and standing very close do not have a sexual connotation. If such behavior makes you uncomfortable, there is no reason why you should not say so and no reason why the other person should not respect your wishes. You should not have to feel uncomfortable, but you should not automatically assume that the behavior means to the other person what it means to you. Conversely, what is a simple gesture of support or friendship to you might make someone else feel uncomfortable. Mutual respect and understanding go a long way toward avoiding problems.

Unfortunately, this approach does not work with everyone. If a coworker does not honor your request, you should begin to document the unwanted behavior. The key steps are (1) let the person know that the continued behavior is unwanted, (2) document the problem, (3) look for corroboration, and, if being straightforward with the offender does not help, (4) follow appropriate legal and company procedures.

If a subordinate comes to you with a complaint, you should begin by assuring your subordinate that you take the complaint seriously and want to cooperate in resolving the matter. Understand that coming to you was not an easy step, and so it is important to begin by showing the subordinate respect and a desire to cooperate. All legal and company procedures must be followed. If the procedures permit, see if there is any possible room for misunderstanding, and, if so, make sure that the people involved talk to each other in a nonthreatening context. Protect the complainer against possible retaliation. If the parties cannot work out the problem between themselves, investigate as fairly, sympathetically, and rigorously as possible. The investigation must be kept confidential—remember that serious harm may come to either the purported victim or the purported harasser if word leaks out. You should be sure to send two messages to everyone involved: first, harassment will not be tolerated, and, second, both parties will be treated fairly and justly. If you determine that the complaint was justified (or might well be justified), try to give the complainer some choice about what happens. Remember that one effect of being harassed is feeling powerless, and so an edict from on high is less satisfactory than a solution in which the victim has had some choice.

Hiring Practices

Ethical hiring requires a balance between judgment and fair rules. Many important factors are hard to measure, such as integrity, loyalty, motivation, and ability to work with others. These are legitimate and important criteria. However, the hiring agent must be careful not to let biases, prejudices, and superficial appearances shape her assessment of these qualities.

Constructing a detailed job description is one tactic that helps ensure fairness in hiring. Milton Snoeyenbos and Robert Almeder cite two reasons for drawing up a detailed job description. First, job descriptions are often required by law. "More fundamentally, utility for the firm and fairness to the prospective employee are enhanced when the employee knows what is expected of him."[17] Nevertheless, the value of a job description must be balanced against the more flexible demands of community. Providing job interviewers with a detailed description of the position to be filled helps to ensure that the factors considered by interviewers are relevant to the job and makes it easier for engineers to be clear about what they must do to succeed. But in a community atmosphere, engineers do what they can to help the project rather than limit their contributions to what is in their job descriptions. In short, job descriptions tend to promote rigidity and compartmentalization instead of teamwork, flexibility, and initiative. Perhaps the best compromise would be drawing up a job description that leaves room for flexibility without being overly vague. For example, the job description might clearly spell out some duties but include a clause that the employer expects the engineer to contribute in every appropriate way to the success of the company or firm. This kind of job description tends to favor the employer. Since job descriptions should be mutually beneficial, job descriptions should also include some things the company or firm owes the employee.

Gary Dessler suggests that interviewers be properly trained and carefully selected, possess a detailed job description, draw their questions from a structured set of guidelines, take care to avoid premature decisions, and supplement interviews with documentable tools such as reference checks and tests. In addition, the tools and techniques the interviewers employ should be validated (documented to be valid predictors of job success).[18]

Again, it must be remembered that hiring decisions demonstrate a conflict between rules and judgment on the one hand, and fairness and community on the other. While testing serves as a check against interviewer bias and helps in protecting hiring agents against legal action, too much reliance on testing results in poor hiring decisions.

It hardly needs to be said that engineers must conduct interviews and make hiring decisions in strict conformance with any relevant laws.

Interdepartmental Dealings and Hiring away from Another Firm

In dealing with another department within the firm or company, a balance must be struck between mutual concern and respect for autonomy. On the one hand, loyalty means that every department has a stake in the flourishing of every other department: all departments are members of the same team. On the other hand, no department will function smoothly unless other departments respect the channels within a department. The question to ask yourself is "Would doing this undermine the orderly functioning of the other department?"

In engineering, companies and firms maintain a kind of gentleperson's agreement that they will not hire engineers away from other companies and firms. To some extent, this serves the companies and firms, since they do not have to compete for the services of top engineers and cannot be as easily manipulated by engineers seeking to play one company against another. There is, however, a legitimate ethical reason for this agreement. The impossibility of drawing a clear line between trade secrets and an engineer's general knowledge raises ethical problems when engineers change jobs. It is difficult for a human resources officer, however ethical, to be sure she is recruiting engineer Smith of P Corporation for his general knowledge and ability rather than for his familiarity with P Corporation's trade secrets and current research. Thus, hiring agents should prefer not to recruit engineers from another firm.

Nevertheless, emergencies may arise in which a company or firm desperately needs a particular kind of skill (not a trade secret) or when an engineer who is underutilized at his current firm would be perfect for a more responsible position in another firm. In such cases, companies have used one of two approaches. When Michaels of Z Company wishes to hire Smith of X Company, Michaels might speak to Smith's supervisor at X Company rather than to Smith himself. The other possibility (more commonly encountered) is for Michaels to mention to a common acquaintance, Jones, that the position at Z Company is available and leave it to Jones to inform Smith. This approach preserves the fiction that Michaels has not contacted or recruited Smith. This example illustrates that flexible rules can still be very useful. An overly strict rule against ''hiring away'' would not be as useful, since firms could not meet urgent needs. However, an overly lax rule would result in constant raiding and hiring away, creating problems of instability and confidentiality. The actual practice, which makes it difficult and cumbersome but not impossible to recruit engineers in other firms, ensures that hiring away does not occur except in cases of special need, the arrangement that best suits most firms.

Illustrating Cases:

Case 46: What guidelines govern the acceptance of additional employment outside of office hours? Consider these factors:

1. the potential conflict of interest between the two employers
2. the effects of informing both employers
3. the extent to which having a second job interferes with wholehearted performance of the first (by tiring the employee, leading to burnout or reduced effectiveness; by cutting into time for further study, community involvement, and dreaming up new ideas; by mitigating social and professional allegiances; and so forth)
4. the degree to which the employer's perception of a ''moonlighting'' employee will harm that employee's career

Case 47: To what extent is personal conduct not directly related to employment duties a valid reason for dismissal? Consider these factors:

1. conduct that embarrasses the company, such as committing adultery; taking an unpopular public stand on issues outside of engineering; gambling, drinking, or using drugs outside the office; committing crimes not related to job activities, such as non-job-related insider trading, running a house of ill-repute, or carrying a gun without a license where that is illegal
2. conduct in the workplace not specifically job-related, such as acting in a conceited manner toward other employees or borrowing and not returning money or articles from other employees

Discussion: Two opposing factors operate here. The communal character of the profession and the company pulls in one direction, while due process and the autonomy of the individual pull in the other.

A few remarks might prove helpful. In the discussion of dealing with subordinates, I noted that employers must not punish employees for conducting outside activities of their choice. Recall also the importance of respecting rights. No employer should place a ''chilling effect'' on the exercise of basic freedoms such as freedom of speech, political association, and assembly. These freedoms are essential to our democratic way of life, and so employers must be sensitive to any pressure they may place upon employees not to exercise these rights freely. An employee's taking an unpopular stand or engaging in a lifestyle found repugnant by supervisors or other employees must not be allowed to affect adversely (or be seen by the employee as adversely affecting) the employee's career. If, as a result, the profession or the company loses some public esteem, that is the price it must pay to operate in a free society. A company may not, without further evidence, assume that an employee who carries a gun without a license will be careless at work or fail to observe the law scrupulously. To do so would be to convict the employee of crimes she did not commit, on flimsy evidence, in a way that denies the employee the opportunity to speak in her own behalf.

Nonetheless, a successful and ethical company is founded on mutual trust and community. The employee in many ways acts as the legal agent of the company, and the company takes the responsibility for ensuring and overseeing the employee's probity in job-related matters. A responsible company will not endanger the public by giving responsibility for a project (or an aspect of a project) to an employee whose judgment, the company has reason to believe, is distorted. So the company may legitimately express concern if an employee with a responsible position is often drunk outside of office hours, has a drug problem, or abuses his or her spouse or children. Indeed, the community model suggests that the company might be a partner in dealing with these problems. Thus, when basic freedoms are not involved, the company may reprimand the employee for, and require the employee to correct, situations that compromise professional values or the community atmosphere, such as not returning borrowed items or failing to treat other employees with respect and comradeship. The company may take special steps, if it seems appropriate, to monitor the activities of those employees whose outside behavior casts doubt on their probity, to warn those employees that strict observance of the law in work-related matters is mandatory, and to provide assistance and counselling where appropriate. When the outside behavior is both well-documented and of such a nature as to cast severe doubt on the engineer's ability to act safely and responsibly, suspension or dismissal may be necessary. (Of course, it is necessary to give the employee a fair hearing before taking detrimental action.)

Case 48: Must a discharged engineer be apprised of the reasons for her dismissal? How frank and detailed must the employer be, and how should the matter be handled?

Discussion: One of the rules in "Dealing with Subordinates" earlier in this chapter indicates that she must be given a frank answer. The principles of treating others fairly, maintaining the values of the engineering profession, and creating a community atmosphere all require that the employer should be as frank as possible in informing employees of the reasons for their dismissal. Vagueness fosters mistrust, and only by being frank can an employer help an employee improve. In a few cases, frankness may even lead to the elimination of a misunderstanding that renders the dismissal unnecessary. "In all justice, an employee is entitled to know in what respect or respects he fails to be satisfactory. A proper explanation may well assist him in altering his attitude to the end that he becomes a valued employee."[19]

Case 49: You need an engineer with knowledge, skill, and experience fitting profile P. A friend of yours tells you that Smith, an engineer with firm Y, fits profile P quite well, and that Smith is somewhat unhappy with Y. Do you make use of this information? Do you approach Smith, and if so, how?

Case 50: Garcia, before her transfer, was the well-liked and respected head of Department P. Of late the employees in Department P have been telling her that her successor, Adams, routinely puts down employees, does not listen to suggestions, makes arbitrary decisions, and does not let anyone else in P know what is going on. What, if anything, should Garcia do?

Discussion: Although Department P is no longer her department, Garcia will not simply ignore the problem if she does have the interests of the company at heart. Insofar as she is able to do so, she certainly ought to be a "sounding board" for her former employees. Nevertheless, it would be not only bad management, but also a violation of community and fairness, for Garcia to foster further discontent in Department P or to complain about Adams to Adams' superior. Rather, Garcia ought to be a voice for a community atmosphere and for treating people fairly and well. The proper course is to (1) to be a sympathetic listener without suggesting that Adams is no good, (2) remind the employees in Department P that they have to work with Adams and that a constructive attitude is more helpful than resentment, and (3) suggest that the employees in Department P speak frankly with Adams about the problems and try to work them out. If these steps do not help, then Garcia may volunteer to take Adams to lunch and, as sympathetically as possible, explain the problems to him and indicate a willingness to help. If, after all this is done, Adams continues his ways, Garcia may counsel the employees in Department P about how to proceed. (See the next case for supplementary details.)

Case 51: Adams, the head of Department P, routinely puts down employees, does not listen to suggestions, makes arbitrary decisions, and does not let anyone else in P know what is going on. The employees in P have made several good-faith attempts to speak with Adams about these problems, but to no avail. The former head of Department P has spoken to Adams informally about these problems, but Adams insists, "It's my department, and nobody is going to tell me how to run it." What should the employees do?

Discussion: Every good-faith effort has already been made to treat Adams fairly and well and to handle the matter informally in a cooperative way. If the company is generally trustworthy, the employees ought to sign a statement articulating their discontents and noting the steps previously taken to correct the problem. They should give a copy of this statement to Adams, indicating that if nothing is done, or if Adams retaliates against those who signed the statement, a copy of the statement will be sent to Adams' superiors. This should not harm the employees: if the company is well run, Adams' superiors will not regard the signers as "troublemakers," since (1) many members of the department signed the statement, which indicates that the problem is real, (2) the statement points out that the employees undertook many informal and constructive steps before they complained to Adams' superiors, and (3) if the complaint is true, it is in the company's interests to do something about the situation.

8

Special Issues in Consulting Engineering

Consulting engineers face special ethical problems. An engineer who works for Boeing or Exxon does not have to compete for clients or advertise his services. Most of the time, his company has control over most aspects of the project on which he is working, and so he must answer primarily to one employer. Consulting engineers, however, usually collaborate with other firms, companies, or agencies. For a particular project, the X corporation may employ firm Y, which in turn subcontracts work to Z consultants, which employs mechanical engineer Jones. Jones must address the needs of X, Y, and Z, whose interests may conflict. This chapter helps you untangle some of the knotty problems that confront consulting engineers.

Advertising

Before 1976, many professional codes prohibited advertising. The Supreme Court ruled in 1976 that such blanket bans on professional advertising were unconstitutional because they restrained trade. As a result, professional societies no longer ban advertising. Instead, they seek to establish guidelines for improper forms of advertising. These fall into two categories: advertisements of questionable honesty, and advertisements that demean the profession of engineering.

Dishonest or Misleading Advertising

Because engineering is built upon trust, consulting engineers have an institutional duty to be scrupulously honest in attracting clients. This duty goes beyond not telling lies. The consulting engineer must avoid, as much as possible, creating a false impression of the capacity, expertise, experience, personnel, or facilities of the firm.

The criteria for honesty are threefold. First, is the information given strictly true? Consulting engineers should scrupulously avoid making any statements that are not strictly true. Second, does the information presented provide a legitimate reason for clients to select the firm? Since the point of advertising is to give clients a reasonable basis for making a choice, consulting engineers should do their best to present clients with information that furnishes legitimate reasons for considering their firm. Third, would the information presented give a false or misleading impression to a reasonable client? Any statement could be misconstrued, while even the most misleading statement, if it is not strictly false, might be understood correctly. The engineer must ask himself, "How would a reasonable client understand this statement?"

It may be useful to look at a few examples of dishonest advertising. It is dishonest to use the names, experience, or achievements of engineers who no longer work for the firm. Of course, care must be used in distinguishing between the personal achievements of prior employees or partners, which may not be used, and the projects handled by prior employees or partners while they were with the firm, which may be mentioned. Thus, it is improper to say "Our engineers have won the X award" when the engineer who won the X award no longer works for the firm. However, it is not improper for the firm to list Y project among its achievements even though the engineer who worked on Y project for the firm no longer works there. Another form of dishonesty consists of exaggerating, explicitly or by insinuation, the role played by the firm in a particular project. If the firm played a minor role in project Y, it is misleading simply to list project Y among the firm's achievements, as this falsely suggests the firm had primary responsibility for project Y. (A reasonable client might have this false impression.) However, it is not improper to say that the firm participated in or assisted in project Y, since the "vote of confidence" given to the firm when its assistance was requested is a legitimate reason for considering the firm. Finally, it is dishonest to list an area or function the firm is not fully qualified to handle. For example, it is improper for a firm to take out an advertisement in the yellow pages suggesting that it conducts site and risk assessments as well as hydrographic surveys, when all hydrographic surveys are subcontracted out and the firm has neither the personnel nor the facilities to carry out any but the simplest site and risk assessment assignments.

Unseemly or Demeaning Advertising

Advertising by consulting engineers should maintain the dignity and high social values of the engineering profession. Engineers should remember that their advertisements represent engineering to the public, and they should avoid advertisements that undercut the values of the engineering profession.

For example, it is inappropriate for consulting engineers to advertise by cost alone. Although price is one legitimate factor in selecting a consulting engineer, advertising that suggests to clients that price is the only factor undermines crucial values of the engineering profession, such as the values of safety, excellence, and thoroughness.

' Providing irrelevant information in an advertisement is also inappropriate. Clients should choose consulting firms on the basis of relevant and defensible values, such as expertise, safety, excellence, experience, and so forth. The profession as a whole is harmed when other factors become the basis of choice. Thus, for example, it would be improper to advertise that the firm's engineers were born locally, since this is not a relevant criterion.

In addition, advertisements whose tone demeans the profession are unseemly. Advertisements represent the profession to the public. Advertisements that are brash, tasteless, or undignified demean the profession in the public's eyes and should be avoided.

Competing with Other Firms

Competitive Bidding

Before 1978, most professional codes and many regulatory boards banned competitive bidding based on price. Although the Supreme Court ruled in 1978 that such bans were unconstitutional, some loopholes remain. Engineers should check local laws and regulations before entering such bids.[1]

Ethically, the key issue is whether such bids undermine professional values. It is improper for consulting engineers to sacrifice quality, safety, care, and excellence to put together a price-competitive bid.

Contingency Fees

The key element here is making sure that you do not compromise your professional judgment. Avoid situations in which you stand to benefit from one result rather than another. For example, suppose you are asked to make a safety or feasibility assessment of a project, knowing that you will probably get the job if the client decides to go ahead with the project. It is hard to turn in a negative report, knowing that this will cost you the project. Similarly, if you are hired to review a project, knowing that you will be paid only if you save the company money, there is a built-in incentive to sacrifice safety to cost.

Bribes and Kickbacks

Kickbacks or bribes to or from state officials or individual corporate officers are absolutely forbidden. Some firms enter into mutual referral arrangements (you recommend me and I will recommend you) or offer discounts or commissions to firms that recommend or refer them. Avoid these mutual referral arrangements unless the situation does not compromise professional judgment and the client knows of the arrangement. Discounts should be passed on to the client.

Derogatory Remarks about Other Engineers

In general, it is both unethical and bad practice to make derogatory remarks about another engineer or engineering firm. If you know a particular engineer or firm to be incompetent or unqualified for a particular kind of task in which it seeks to engage, taking formal action may be appropriate or even morally required but only after speaking to the individual or firm in question. "Informal" derogatory remarks are unfair, since they give the victim no opportunity to explain or defend himself. If, when reviewing the work of another engineer, you find flaws, inaccuracies, or safety problems, or you can devise a more efficient solution, you should make your recommendation in a way that does not unnecessarily reflect badly on the other engineer.

Reviewing the Work of Others

Reviewing the Work of Unlicensed Individuals

Is it ethical for an engineer to review, check, and stamp plans or designs of an unlicensed individual when those plans were not prepared under the engineer's supervision?

In many cases this would violate state or local laws or regulations. Make sure that no applicable local laws are being violated, either in letter or in spirit. Even if this practice is legal in your area, nonetheless some purely ethical constraints should discourage you from reviewing, checking, and stamping such work.

In some special situations, a licensed individual may legitimately seek the stamp of an unlicensed engineer. For example, a small church may need a new facility but be unable to build the facility without substantial volunteer work. One of its members, though unlicensed, is competent to design the facility. The church group wishes to employ a licensed engineer to review, check, and stamp the member's plans. Of course, it is always unethical to assist an unlicensed individual in carrying on an engineering practice in violation of the spirit of the licensing laws.

If the individual who drew up the plans is not the original client, the engineer should consult the original client before stamping to make sure that the client understands and approves of the arrangement and that the final plans continue to suit the client's needs.

The complexity and potential risk involved in the plans is an important factor. The greater the complexity or potential risk involved, the more an engineer ought to hesitate before reviewing, checking, and stamping work not prepared under her supervision.

In any case, before stamping, the engineer ought to check the work as thoroughly as if it were her own, since she is assuming responsibility for the work.

Reviewing the Work of Other Engineers

In many circumstances it is both ethical and sensible for a client to ask another consulting engineer to review the work of the original engineer, for example, in the event of a physical failure or when plans are substantially complete but the client believes the plans are deficient or uneconomical.

The reviewing engineer should not overemphasize minor objections and should not hesitate to commend the original engineer's work when warranted. Nevertheless, serious drawbacks should be clearly documented. When feasible, the original engineer should be notified of the review and, if the client consents, be given a copy of the reviewing engineer's report.

Safety and Liability

Consulting firms face special problems of legal liability for jobs with which they are associated. For example, in *Krieger v. J.E. Greiner & Co., Inc. et al.,* reviewed in the Maryland Court of Appeals in 1978, the court ruled that because the engineering consultant had previously inspected the work site for safety, this could be taken as conduct indicating that the consultant is responsible for supervising the safety of the work. As a result of this ruling, consultants are sometimes reluctant to do any extracontractual inspection, even though such inspections sometimes prevent disasters. To limit this problem, make sure the contract is clear about responsibilities.

APPENDIXES

Appendix 1

Two Sample Suggestions

*Formation of an Environmental and Community
Issues Advisory Board*

The purpose of the Environmental and Community
Issues Advisory Board (ECIAB) is to include citizens in the
process of making decisions that affect community interests
(such as the environment, safety, and so forth), since community values are an important factor in making such decisions
ethically. The ECIAB is advisory only, so its deliberations
should be full, frank, informed, and free of company pressure.
Its job is not to make technical assessments but to speak for
community values in the decision-making process. The
advice of the ECIAB, while not determinative, provides
important input to the company in making its decisions. To
meet this goal, the ECIAB must include representatives of the
entire spectrum of the community. Moreover, special efforts
should be make to represent groups likely to object to the
company's decisions. However, frankness is feasible only if
the members of the ECIAB understand the importance of
keeping confidential the sensitive information they are given
and if they can be trusted not to violate the demands of
confidentiality.

A viable ECIAB might include a state representative, a
member of the clergy, a representative of a parents' group, a
company engineer, a representative of an environmental

group, a representative of an animal rights group, a representative of the business community, and representative citizens from the full range of socioeconomic, ethnic, and religious segments of the region. This list is tentative and should be tailored to fit the particular circumstances of the region. (For example, if the region affected consists of a city surrounded by farms, both the urban and rural populations should be represented).

Ethical Ombudsperson

The company should employ an individual with special training in ethics who is independent of all other chains of command. The ombudsperson's role is to give advice to anyone in the company who seeks it and to speak up for ethical considerations in any matter affecting the company. The independence of the ombudsperson is crucial, for only so can any member of the company feel free to consult the ombudsperson fully and frankly about any ethical problem that might arise, without fear of reprisal or negative consequences, and only so can the ombudsperson feel fully free to speak frankly and forcefully. Again, the ombudsperson's role is advisory: the ombudsperson has no decision-making power. However, the opinions and arguments of a well-trained and respected ombudsperson will have considerable weight.

Additional duties of the ombudsperson might include running training sessions on ethics for the company and publication and professional activity in areas of professional ethics.

Appendix 2

Summary of Key Points

Chapter 1

- Many of the ethical decisions that individual engineers must make are not settled by rules
    Rules do not cover every situation
    Rules require interpretation in a way that is not always obvious
- The values implicit in rules and executive decisions should be widely understood and discussed within the organization
    Companies and firms flourish when their people have common values
    Without communication between all levels of an organization, ethical problems may slip between the cracks
    Large decisions often result from many small decisions at different levels
    Firms make better decisions when all engineers can provide free and informed input
- Engineers who understand the moral basis of the rules have a greater motivation to obey them
- The corporate climate is determined by people who advance in the corporation, who tend to take with them the attitudes they learned before being promoted
- Engineers who understand the ethical dimension of engineering are better and happier engineers

233

- Ethics is good business
     - While acting ethically often costs more in the short run, acting unethically usually costs more in the long run. The benefits of ethical conduct are often long-term and hard to calculate
     - Companies and consulting firms who can show a strong ethical awareness will increasingly be more marketable
     - Ethics makes for better and more productive engineers
- A partnership between engineers and environmentalists, based on mutual understanding, is more productive than an adversarial relationship
- The ethical profile of a company depends not only on the rules set by upper-level executives, but also on the ethical outlook and understanding of each and every employee
- It is better to work in a community workplace than in a cut-throat workplace
- The life of values is better than the consumer life, since the consumer life is necessarily isolated, unhappy, and trivial

Chapter 2

- Making ethical decisions consists of

Step 1. Identifying your options
Step 2. Identifying the relevant moral considerations
Step 3. Determining how these considerations apply to your case
Step 4. Determining how these moral considerations should be weighed for this situation
Step 5. Calculating the result

Chapter 3

- Technology is practical wisdom
    - Technology reflects human nature
        - ——The distinctive human attribute is the ability to reshape the world in line with our dreams and visions
        - ——Human beings are by nature rational animals
    - Technology is committed to reshaping the world rationally, to maintaining a partnership with nature, and to establishing a sense of community
- Technology is not value-neutral: it is the search for human excellence
- Engineering may be defined as the safe advancement of the progress of the human community, in partnership with nature, through know-how used in a systematic practice of clear, clean, practical decision making
- Values of the engineering profession include
    - Safety
    - Human progress
        - ——Knowledge
        - ——Welfare
    - Clean, clear decision making
        - ——Precision
        - ——Clarity
        - ——Ingenuity and creativity
        - ——The value of excellence generally
        - ——Concentration and care
    - Community
    - Partnership with nature
- Determining the extent of a risk involves asking these questions:

How severe is the possible harm to each individual?

How widespread is the danger?

How likely is the danger?

- Balancing risks against benefits involves the following guides:

    Seek the lowest likelihood of harm multiplied by the total possible harm

    When in doubt, be conservative

    Would you be willing to have your family undergo this risk for these benefits?

    Opt for solutions somewhat less risky than the economically optimal point

    Be a good trustee of the public welfare: exercise slightly more caution on the behalf of others than you would exercise for yourself

- Determining the nature of risks relies on these questions:

    Is the risk voluntarily taken?

    Do those at risk know the potential risks?

    Do those at risk reap the benefits of the risk?

- To determine whether to publicize risks, ask the following questions:

    Is there a legal duty to publicize the risk?

    Can the community take action to reduce the risk?

    How great is the risk?

    Are there legitimate reasons for withholding the information?

    How much will the company be hurt by publicizing the risk?

- A community is a group of mutually interested persons working out a joint moral vision through common institutions, practices, and relationships, all of which are dedicated to that vision

- Make sure that the special qualities of the natural world are not destroyed

- When building or remaking the world, be sensitive to the beauty of nature
- Make sure that our remaking of the world is no more intrusive than necessary
- Three types of solutions to an environmental problem are
    Technical modifications of a process
    Alternate technologies
    Nontechnological solutions
- Responses to an environmental problem include the following:
    Seek an alternative product or process
    Develop and publicize an additional product, process, or method of use that minimizes the harmful effects
    Publicize the problem and encourage solutions
    Take the product or process off the market, a step indicated by the answers to the following questions:
    ——How bad is the problem?
    ——How much would the company suffer?
    ——Would removal do any good?

Chapter 4

- One may be required to fight a battle
    As a matter of principle
    As a matter of responsibility
    As a practical matter
    Because there is no neutral option
- When deciding which battles to fight, ask the following questions:
    How bad is the infraction?
    ——What are the expected consequences of the infraction?

——What is the moral character of the infraction?

What is the expected cost to me (and to other nonguilty parties)?

To what extent am I implicated?

——Am I in a special position to know about or correct the problem?

——Have I close ties to the infracting organization?

——Have I played a role in the infraction itself?

——Would overlooking the infraction compromise my doing my job faithfully?

- Be straightforward
- Be impartial, that is

     Give the person a chance to present his side

     Do not jump to conclusions

     Do not let your personal feelings for or against someone cloud your judgment

     Judge on the basis of facts and sound evidence, not superficial appearances

     Observe the principle of just deserts

- Do not exploit or manipulate
- Help each person to make the most of him- or herself

     Allow scope for individual differences

     Maximize opportunity for growth and taking responsibility

     Encourage feedback and thoughtful participation

     Reward and encourage effort, achievement, and commitment

     Be patient but firm

- Build a community atmosphere
- Respect the rights of others
- The only life worth living is the life committed to values, and you betray that commitment if you do not do your best to leave the world no worse than you found it
- Always treat people as ends, never merely as means

Do not use people

Treat others with dignity and respect

- Engineers must be scrupulous about observing legal rights and should be sensitive to moral rights
- Engineers must treat people as having special value and must respect other people's desire to make decisions for themselves
- Principles of institutional responsibility include the following:

    You are responsible for seeing to it that your participation in a project, in your company, in the profession, and in society generally supports and leads to an ethical outcome

    You are responsible for monitoring, to the best of your ability, the ethical character of your company, profession, and society and for taking whatever steps are warranted when your company, profession, or society goes astray

- The institutional duties of engineering mean that engineers become obligated to give greater weight to the pursuit of safety and welfare than other people must
- Engineers have a special institutional duty to perform thorough and reliable tests and keep accurate and precise records of those tests, to respect nature, to use technological know-how to further human welfare, and to obey legal requirements, both in letter and in spirit
- Features of a profession include

    Extensive training

    A significant intellectual component

    Providing an important service in society

    A process of certification or licensure

    An organization of members to promote the goals of the profession and the economic well-being of its members

Room for autonomy in one's work

An institution that functions because of public trust

- Consequences of these features:

> Because professionals have a coercive bargaining position, professionals are morally required to exercise restraint in what they demand in exchange for their services and have a moral obligation to look out for the public interest, since those adversely affected by engineering projects are not always in a position to bargain effectively

> Because of the need for professional self-regulation, engineering as a profession has a special duty to regulate the competence and ethics of practicing engineers. For the individual engineer, this means participating in professional societies. It means taking some responsibility to see that incompetent or unethical colleagues do no harm. This may mean reporting them, not "covering up" for them, or simply speaking to them

> Engineers owe a debt of gratitude to society, and so they have a special duty to be good public citizens and to use their skills for the public good

- Since an engineer is a "social enabler and catalyst," an engineer who, because of her expertise, has a special perspective on public issues should make her voice heard
- The public must be involved in important engineering decisions that affect the life of the community
- In promoting good consequences, one must sometimes evaluate the consequences of particular actions and sometimes evaluate the consequences of policies
- Factors that count toward thinking in terms of policy include the following:

> People must be able to form secure expectations

Treating each case individually would lead to unfairness

The thing in question is important to the institutional
character of the professional or corporate setting

• Factors that count toward thinking in terms of particular acts
include the following:

Cases are substantially different from one another

The harm or unfairness in a particular case outweighs
the benefits of a policy

• Two factors that set limits on promoting good consequences
are

It is important to be part of a moral community

You should live in a way that proclaims your values
and ideals

• A relevant moral question is ''What if everyone did that?''

• Engineers must show great concern for truth and honesty

Engineers must place a high value on keeping their
promises

——Promises should not be made lightly

——Only a strong duty or value can outweigh the
duty to keep a promise

——When a promise cannot be kept, the promisee is
due something

Engineers must not engage in dubious transactions

Minor obligations must be subordinated to more
pressing ones. How pressing the duty to keep your
promises is depends on the nature and importance
of the promise: the more formal and solemn the
promise, and the more harmful the consequences
of breaking the promise, the more pressing is the
obligation to keep the promise

Duties may be allocated as long as the allocated tasks
are being properly performed

- In making ethical decisions you may draw upon
  - Examples of good moral decisions you can try to emulate
  - Hard cases that raise tough questions
  - Pure cases that set the problem clearly
- To understand the meaning of our actions, we must think about how they affect others
- We must take very seriously the way we affect others
- Questions to ask in thinking about when to break the rules are
  - To what extent is the practice rule-dependent?
  - How central to the practice is this rule?
  - ——To what extent would the practice be recognizable without this rule?
  - ——How important to the practice is standardizing this aspect?
  - ——What kind of rule is it, i.e., one without which the practice could not exist, one that governs the tone and public role of the profession, or one that encourages ease of communication and cooperation?
  - How does keeping the rule in this case relate to the point of the rule?
  - How does the value of the point or aim of the practice measure against the harm caused by following the rules?
  - How unfair would it be to others if this case were treated differently?
  - ——Would there be any real unfairness if not all cases are treated alike in this regard?
  - ——How sensitive to the appearance of irregularity is the situation? Strict uniformity is more important in conflictful than in cooperative situations, in

formal than in informal settings, and in public than
in private settings
• When in doubt, follow the rule

Chapter 5

• Relevant factors when deciding whether to blow the whistle
include the following:
> There is a clear harm to society
>> ——How bad is it (morally and in terms of the
>> likelihood, severity, and widespread nature of the
>> risk)?
>> ——Does a neutral option exist?
> The whistleblower's proximity to the situation places
> him or her in the position to report the company;
> relevant questions include
>> ——How directly am I involved?
>> ——Am I involved in the infraction?
>> ——Am I closely tied to the infracting organization?
>> ——Would doing nothing compromise my doing my
>> job faithfully?
> There is some chance of succeeding
> No one else is more able to blow the whistle and more
> proximate. Ask yourself, "Am I in a special
> position to know about or correct the problem?"
> All avenues within the company have been exhausted
> The employee has documentation of the problem.
> Document everything, including your attempts to
> fix the problem within the company
> The employee has good reason to believe that whis-
> tleblowing will bring about the necessary changes
> to safeguard the public

Releasing confidential information without your employer's consent is permissible only when every attempt has been made to obtain the employer's consent and it is absolutely necessary to document extreme and severe danger to the public, serious violations of the law, or grossly immoral conduct

Would an anonymous "leak" would be effective in solving the problem?

Would the leak remain anonymous?

Can I afford to go public?

- Do not work for unethical firms or companies
- Deal with potential problem situations early
- Suggest that your firm or company establish troubleshooting mechanisms for dealing with such problems
- Engineers must make every effort to be as competent as possible

Read trade and professional books and journals

Attend professional meetings, workshops, and seminars

Take additional courses or other training

Make the most of work opportunities. Ask questions, try to understand all the decisions pertinent to your project, speak to colleagues about what they are doing, try new things

Make every effort to be at your best

——Avoid coming to work tired

——Do not let personal troubles interfere with your work

——Take care of your health, both mental and physical

- Engineers should never undertake a task or responsibility beyond their competence

Be candid about your own limitations

When you need assistance, ask for it

- Engineers must not falsify records or break the law
- Engineers should be faithful to the spirit as well as the letter of the law
- Engineers must be scrupulous in avoiding the appearance of impropriety; never say or write anything you would not wish to explain in court

  Everything you say or write could conceivably wind up in court

  Think of yourself as an ''ambassador'' for your company

  Be particularly careful in anything touching on discrimination. Give extra thought to every remark or memo that might be construed as expressing a bias concerning race, gender, national origin, sexual orientation, or religion

  Avoid using terms or phrases that might suggest either power to control or collusion in controlling market factors

  Avoid using terms or phrases that might suggest less than strict and voluntary compliance with laws and regulations
- Be a (faithful) consulting rather than an adversarial salesperson

Chapter 6

- To the extent feasible, avoid situations that might bias, or appear to others to bias, one's judgment on the firm's or company's behalf, including the following:

  Engaging in activities that compete with the company. This would include owning stock in competing firms or companies and marketing a product that competes with the company's product

Having a relationship with suppliers that may compromise judgment. This would include accepting gifts with more than nominal value (often set at $25), accepting extravagant entertainment or special discounts not available to other members of the company, accepting cash payments or loans, moonlighting for suppliers, noncompany business transactions with suppliers, and owning stock in supplier companies

Conducting business with the company. This would include selling real estate to the company, leasing equipment to the company, and selling engineering, contracting, managerial, or financial services to the company

Controlling company employment relations with relatives, including determining the salary, raises, promotions, or bonuses of close family members

Using firm or company position, facilities, or knowledge of firm or company affairs for personal gain, including speculating on real estate based on inside knowledge of company plans and using company equipment or supplies for personal uses

- When it is not possible to avoid a conflict of interest situation, observe strict impartiality, in appearance and in fact
- Protect five kinds of information:

The privacy of individuals

The integrity of the decision processes

Trade secrets. Consider "1) the extent to which the information is known outside the business; 2) the extent to which it is known by employees and others involved in business; 3) the extent of measures taken to guard the secrecy of the information; 4) the value of the information to holders and to competitors; 5) the amount of effort or money expended in developing the information; 6) the ease or difficulty with which the information could be properly acquired or duplicated by others.''

Business plans

Client information

- Engineers should make every effort to avoid changing companies
- Engineers should not accept employment if they believe the motive for the offer is their knowledge of trade secrets
- Engineers should not explicitly reveal trade secrets and must be very skittish about drawing upon special knowledge paid for by their previous employer
- The general knowledge, skill, and experience an employee gains in his or her job is part of his or her remuneration
- Engineers should seek new approaches to problems they have worked on under a previous employer, rather than seeking to duplicate or make minor variations to secret processes
- Honesty and communication often avoid or resolve problems
- Questions to ask about modifying others' patents include

    Has the innovator had a chance to benefit from the innovation?

    Is the modification a real improvement?

    How significant a change is the modification?

    Is there any doubt about the legality of marketing the modification?

- Seven questions you should ask yourself about a gift include

    What is the value of the gift?

    What is the purpose of the gift?

    What are the circumstances under which the gift was given or received?

What is the position and sensitivity to influence of the
person receiving the gift?

What is the accepted business practice in the area?

What is the company's policy?

What is the law?

Chapter 7

- Three kinds of work relationships are artisan-master, professional status, and protégé-patron
- Questions to ask when balancing the three kinds of work
relationships include

What is the nature of the work I am asked to do?

What is at stake if I give my employing company
what it ought to have, instead of what it wants?

What particular understanding do I have with my
company or firm?

- In dealing with protégés, keep the following factors in mind:

Do not be afraid of giving away something important

Do not just share complaints about the company

Do not look for someone who will humor and praise
you; instead, seek someone who really wants to
learn from you

Seek someone not more than twenty years your
junior

Keep a loose and flexible relationship and realize that
your protégé will have his or her own way of doing
things

If the relationship feels like a drain or a chore, the
pairing is a mistake

Remember that the relationship should be a two-way
street

• In dealing with subordinates, observe the following factors:
  Do not assign repetitive work to the same employee
  Recognition awards should not be a substitute for a simple "Well done"
  In the case of inadequate performance, inform the employee constructively
  When firing an employee, inform the employee of the specific reasons for the decision
  Encourage and reward membership in and attendance at meetings of technical societies
  Maintain a neat and attractive office environment
  Work from the highest common purposes possible while not overlooking the economic motive
  Remember that an employee's need for a good self-image is often as important as economic needs
  Do not discriminate against an employee for criticizing the organization
  Do not discriminate against an employee for outside activities that do not violate the engineer's duties as an engineer or an employee
  Do not discharge or penalize without a fair hearing an employee who alleges in good faith that his or her rights have been violated
  Follow faithfully all legal requirements and company policies
  Follow strict rules of nonfraternization when
  ——The context is highly competitive
  ——The perception of impartiality is a central goal of the activity
  ——Building walls between the people involved does not undermine a central task
  Otherwise strive for a community atmosphere, taking special care to establish trust in your integrity

Chapter 8

- Do not use unseemly or dishonest advertising, such as
    - Using the names, experience, or achievements of engineers who are no longer employed by the firm
    - Exaggerating the role played by the firm in a particular project
    - Listing an area or function the firm is not fully qualified to handle
    - Advertising by cost alone
    - Advertisements whose tone demeans the profession
    - Providing irrelevant information
    - Questions to ask of advertisements include
        - ——Is the information given strictly true?
        - ——Does the information presented provide a legitimate reason for clients to select the firm?
        - ——Would the information give a false or misleading impression to a reasonable client?
- Do not accept bribes or kickbacks
- Do not make unnecessary derogatory remarks about other engineers
- Use care in stamping or reviewing the work of others
- Do not stamp the work of other engineers unless the law permits it, the client knows, and you use the same care in checking that you would with your own work

Notes

1. Cf. Kirk Hanson, "Institutionalizing Ethics in the Corporation," in *Corporate Governance and Institutionalizing Ethics,* ed. W. Michael Hoffman et al., Proceedings of the Fifth National Conference on Business Ethics (Lexington: Lexington Books, 1983), p. 186. He argues, "Not every ethical conflict and concern that will arise can be anticipated. . . . Therefore, it [is important to] establish firmly in all employee's minds a few key values that can be applied to any situation that will arise."

2. John E. Fleming, "Managing the Corporate Ethical Climate," in *Corporate Governance and Institutionalizing Ethics,* ed. W. Michael Hoffman et al., p. 217.

3. Donald G. Jones, ed., *Doing Ethics in Business* (Cambridge, Mass.: Oelgeschlager, Gunn and Hain, 1982), p. 8.

4. Gerald E. Ottoson, "Essentials of an Ethical Corporate Climate," in *Doing Ethics in Business,* ed. Donald G. Jones, p. 155.

5. Cf. R. J. Evans, "Commentary on the Code of Ethics," *Journal of Professional Issues in Engineering* 114 (April 1988): 151: Evans asserts that "ethical statements are about specific situations and . . . these statements can be justified only in the context of the situation." Unfortunately, Evans also insists that "noncognitivism appears to be appropriate

251

for justification of all ethical engineering statements." It seems clear, however, that if we are to set guidelines for ourselves and others to follow, we want a better reason for doing so than "It seems good to me," "I like it," or "That's what most engineers expect."

Chapter 2

1. Cf. K. R. Pavlovic, "Autonomy and Obligation: Is There an Engineering Ethics?" in *Engineering Professionalism and Ethics,* ed. James Schaub and Karl Pavlovic (New York: John Wiley and Sons, 1983), p. 230: Pavlovic states, "If you think you can nicely circumscribe a problem area, the usual next step is either to bring in or manufacture the 'experts,' professionals who will generate the specialized knowledge and then stand ready to supply professional solutions. . . . This approach . . . makes no sense in ethics."

2. For example, an engineer given a legal order by the Nazis to engineer more efficient extermination facilities ought to defy the law.

Chapter 3

1. Samuel Florman, in *The Existential Pleasures of Engineering* (New York: St. Martin's Press, 1976), cites a number of relevant remarks on p. 94. First, the engineer has "a responsibility to help society" by working "for the use and convenience of man" (James R. Killian, Jr.), and the engineer's "opportunity for productive contributions is almost without limit; his obligation to judge wisely and imaginatively is profound" (Newman A. Hall). Moreover, engineering "can provide a life of genuine satisfaction"

(Vannevar Bush), namely, "the deep satisfaction that stems from an understanding of the world in which we live" (George E. Holbrook).

2. Most economists follow the philosopher David Hume in thinking that only means (and not ends) can be evaluated. As a result, they have regarded practical wisdom as wisdom about means, that is, the ability to achieve any given end. Thus, economists have viewed technology simply as the capacity to make outcomes conform to one's will. If, however, as I would argue, ends also are subject to rational scrutiny, then technology applies to the choice of ends as well as to the choice of means, and the means must reflect the values inherent in rational ends.

Unfortunately, space does not permit me to argue for this important claim. However, because this point helps illustrate the nature of ethical reasoning, I suggest that perhaps people have found Hume's view plausible because they have taken too narrow a view of reason. It is true enough that deduction and induction alone will not serve to show that one end is better than another. But neither will deduction and induction alone serve to show that one scientific theory is better than another, as philosophers of science have pointed out. Rather, rational assessment must draw on a wide assortment of tools, none of which is conclusive, but which, together, give some reason for preferring one end to another. Those tools include deduction and induction. They also include what I call "picture building." It counts in favor of a theory that it is not an isolated view but is instead an integral part of a comprehensive picture.

For example, can the values inherent in a particular end be shown to be part of the structure of values upon which our whole way of life is built? Our belief that casual killing of people is wrong, after all, follows from the view that people's projects are important and deserve respect, since corpses rarely are able to pursue their goals. And our entire way of life (e.g., contract law, friendship, and marriage) is based on respecting people's efforts to achieve their goals. So either casual killing of persons is wrong, or our entire way of life is misguided. This is not proof, of course, since our entire way of life might be misguided. But it does provide some support for the view that casual killing of persons is wrong.

By way of contrast, our taboo against consensual incest between adults does not form part of a comprehensive picture of our way of life. There is no value, the respecting of which proscribes consensual incest between adults, that is at the core of human life as we know it.

Arguments of recognition also play an important role in ethical assessment. One way to show the value of X is to describe a form of life based on X in such a way that the hearer recognizes value in that form of life (films and fiction excel at this sort of argument). There are more tools of rational assessment in heaven and earth than are dreamt of in Hume's philosophy.

3. In 1828 Thomas Tredgold defined engineering as "the art of directing the great sources of power in nature for the use and convenience of man" (quoted in Florman, *Existential Pleasures of Engineering,* p. 19). Mike Martin and Roland Schinzinger, in *Ethics in Engineering* (New York: McGraw-Hill, 1983), view engineering as "social experimentation." From this they conclude on page 63 that "the general features of morally responsible engineers [are] . . . a conscientious commitment to live by moral values, a comprehensive perspective, autonomy and accountability [Haydon, Graham, "On Being Responsible," *Philosophical Quarterly* 28 (1978), pp. 46–57]. Or stated in greater detail . . . 1) A primary obligation to protect the safety of and respect the right of consent of human subjects. 2) A constant awareness of the experimental nature of any project, imaginative forecasting of

its possible side effects, and a reasonable effort to monitor them. 3) Autonomous, personal involvement in all steps of a project. 4) Accepting accountability for the results of a project.''

4. This is a "value-based" reason, stemming from the definition of engineering as a profession. Martin and Schinzinger, in *Ethics in Engineering,* mention three "contractual" reasons for thinking engineers have a special obligation to promote safety: by joining a professional society with a safety-based code, by accepting employment, or by entering a career underwritten by the public, engineers tacitly promise to strive for public safety.

5. Even if the automobile saves some lives a year, and even if the number of passengers who die in train accidents would increase if automobile travel were banned, it is patent that many lives would be saved each year were we to give up the automobile.

6. Martin and Schinzinger, in *Ethics in Engineering,* assert on page 97 that "[a] thing is safe (to a certain degree) with respect to a given person or group at a given time if, were they fully aware of its risks and expressing their most settled values, they would judge those risks to be acceptable (to a certain degree).'' This definition is not useful for two reasons. First, the qualifier "to a certain degree" takes the teeth out of the definition—everything is safe to a certain degree (perhaps a very small degree) if it yields any benefit whatsoever. Of course, the authors are really trying to define the *degree* of safety. But this leaves untouched the crucial question, namely, how much safety (so defined) the engineer should seek. More importantly, the definition makes safety relative to the values of a group. To a motorcycle gang, which, let us suppose, does not highly value what the rest of us call "safety," racing on a precipice might turn out to be "safe" by this definition. We need to add, in other words, that the

group's "settled values" are rational ones. But the problem of defining safety is precisely the problem of deciding how much risk it is rational to assume.

7. Martin and Schinzinger, *Ethics in Engineering,* p. 107.

8. David Bazelon, in "Risk and Democracy," *Professional Engineer* 50 (March 1980), states on page 40 that evaluating acceptable risks involves "critical value choices [that] ultimately are reserved for the public." This may be accomplished through government or, more feasibly, through citizen advisory boards.

9. Cf. Marvin L. Manheim, "Values and Professional Practice," in *Values and the Public Works Professional,* proceedings of a workshop for the American Public Works Association, reprinted in *Engineering Professionalism and Ethics,* ed. Schaub and Pavlovic, p. 119: He asserts, "There must be full opportunity for timely and constructive involvement of affected interests in the process, such that every interest—individual or group—[that] may potentially be affected by the changes being considered has full and timely access to all relevant information and has full opportunity to influence the process constructively."

10. Ron Westrum, *Technologies and Society* (Belmont, Calif.: Wadsworth, 1991), pp. 255–56.

11. Information for this example is based on Rogene A. Buchholz, *Fundamental Concepts and Problems in Business Ethics* (Englewood Cliffs, N.J.: Prentice-Hall, 1989), pp. 190–210.

12. Florman, in *Existential Pleasures of Engineering,* points out on page 32 that "failure [in engineering] results from lack of imagination," from carelessness and human error, and from ignorance.

13. Cf. Harvey Gobas, "Professionalism and the Civil Engineer," *Journal of Professional Issues in Engineering*

114 (April 1988): p. 147: "Thou shalt be receptive to new ideas and innovative approaches to old problems."

14. John A. Young, "Technology and Competitiveness: A Key to the Economic Future of the United States," in *Technology and the Future,* ed. Albert H. Teich, 5th ed. (New York: St. Martin's Press, 1990), p. 306.

15. This section contains information on various products and processes, on the effects and amounts of pollution, and so forth. Such information quickly becomes outdated. It is given primarily for the purpose of illustration.

16. For further information on the Aral Sea, see V. M. Kotlyankov, "The Aral Sea: A Critical Environmental Zone," *Environment* 33 (January-February 1991): 4–7.

17. John M. Fowler, *Energy and the Environment,* 2d ed. (New York: McGraw-Hill, 1984). Nitrous oxide in the air also aggravates bronchitis and emphysema and impairs resistance to infection. Sulfuric acid causes respiratory problems, corrosion, and smog.

18. H. Patricia Hynes, *Earth Right* (Rocklin, Calif.: Prima Publishing, 1990), pp. 85–86.

19. Although the idea is not a new one, the invention of Gaia theory is generally credited to James E. Lovelock and Lynn Margulis. Some further books on Gaia theory include J. E. Lovelock, *The Ages of Gaia: A Biography of Our Living Earth* (New York: W. W. Norton and Company, 1988); William Irwin Thompson, ed., *Gaia: A Way of Knowing: Political Implications of the New Biology* (Great Barrington, Mass.: Lindisfarne Press, 1987); and Lynn Margulis and Dorion Sagan, *Microcosmos: Four Billion Years of Microbial Evolution* (New York: Summit Books, 1986).

20. Lawrence E. Joseph, *Gaia: The Growth of an Idea* (New York: St. Martin's Press, 1990), p. 6.

21. Ibid., p. 115.

22. Ibid., p. 2.

23. Ibid., p. 151.

24. Some writers who want the law to recognize the rights of natural objects view their suggestion as a "legal fiction"; they argue that treating trees *as if* they had rights is the best legal means of protecting the environment. Since this is really a legal point rather than an ethical one, I will not discuss this view.

25. More generally, writers have assumed either anthropocentric or geocentric views of nature. Anthropocentric views include John Passmore's claims in *Man's Responsibility for Nature: Ecological Problems and Western Traditions* (London: Duckworth, 1974) that nature has only extrinsic, utilitarian value to people and that proper aesthetic enjoyment of nature derives from seeing human improvements upon natural forms (such as the English garden). Eugene Hargrove in *Foundations of Environmental Ethics* (Englewood Cliffs, N.J.: Prentice-Hall, 1989) describes the early eighteenth-century view of nature as either picturesque (pretty) or sublime (vast). Hargrove says this view gave way to nature as interesting, and peoples' interest in nature centered on the properties of complexity, diversity, variety, individuality, and geological time.

By contrast, a geocentric view regards nature as having intrinsic value apart from all human perceptions, a value to which human values are, ultimately, subordinate. The Transcendentalists took a transitional, if somewhat fuzzy, view: nature is a mirror image of the human soul, and the attitude toward which human beings should aspire is one of unity with nature, which represents human nature in its "pure" form.

I suggest a more synthetic view: nature has meaning in the logical space of human thought. Natural processes in a world without any intelligent beings, such as *homo sapiens,* is a meaningless chatter of subatomic events: one quantum state is as good as another. In this sense, nature has no value apart from human (or humanlike) beings. However, human worldviews create a logical space within which mountains have meaning apart from our perception of them. For example, it requires a human worldview to establish the category of the powerful. Once established, however, the concept of power has application to the natural world whether we see it or not. There is something grand and powerful about Mount Rainier rising above the mists, even if no one ever sees it, and so the mountain's beauty and value does not depend upon our seeing it. Once the categories of meaning exist, the world resonates with meaning: the very stones do prate of value. But without human (or humanlike) consciousness there would be no Mount Rainier. There would just be neutrinos and electrons hopping between quantum states.

The relation between natural processes and human thought is also dynamic: our concepts derive from natural processes at the same time as nature acquires meaning by virtue of those concepts. Just as our concept of human power derives from understanding Mount Rainier, so does the thrill of seeing Mount Rainier derive from a metaphorical view of the great rock as, for example, similar to the deaf Beethoven creating the Ninth Symphony. Moreover, our concepts are reshaped by paying closer attention to natural processes (as happens, for example, in political philosophy, when the body politic is viewed as a kind of ecosystem). In short, the idea of partnership with nature governs even ethics and human consciousness.

26. See Florman, *Existential Pleasures of Engineering,* p. 67: "Does nature consist of farms, seashores, lakes and meadows, to use Reich's list?" Must we not also include, asks Florman, such hostile environments as outer space, ice fields, and deserts? "If farms and meadows are considered 'natural' even though they have been made by men, . . . what is 'unnatural?' "

27. Indeed, in some sense, human procreation itself is a form of human intervention.

28. Steve H. Hanke, *Policy Analysis* 1 (Winter 1975),

cited in Penelope ReVelle and Charles ReVelle, *The Environment* (Willard Grant, 1981).

29. "Business's Green Revolution," *U.S. News and World Report,* February 19, 1990, p. 45.

30. Ibid., pp. 45–46.

31. See A. Myrick Freeman, Robert Haveman, and Allen Kneese, *Economics of Environmental Policy* (New York: John Wiley and Sons, 1973), reprinted, in part, in *Contemporary Issues in Business Ethics,* ed. Joseph R. Desjardins and John J. McCall, 2d ed. (Belmont, Calif.: Wadsworth, 1990), pp. 354–64.

32. Penelope ReVelle and Charles ReVelle, *The Environment* (Willard Grant, 1981), p. 7.

33. Ibid., p. 8.

34. Hynes, *Earth Right.*

35. ReVelle and ReVelle, *The Environment.*

36. Hynes, in *Earth Right,* indicates on page 79 that less than 1 percent of plastics were recycled in 1989, compared to 33 percent of aluminum and 21 percent of paper. However, the Society of the Plastics Industry, cited in *Saving the Earth* on page 127, said that 20 percent of all plastic products made in the United States in 1984 were recycled, compared to 54 percent of aluminum cans. It is doubtful that recycling decreased between 1989 and 1984. More likely, the difference is due to the way in which figures were gathered, what is counted as a plastic product, and so forth. This example alone shows that one must be cautious about relying on recycling statistics, especially in the absence of detailed information about how the statistic was determined.

37. Will Steger and John Bowermaster, *Saving the Earth* (New York: Knopf, 1990).

38. Hynes, *Earth Right.*

39. Thomas H. Maugh II, "Hazardous Wastes Technology Is Available," *Science* 204 (June 1979).

40. Ibid. According to Maugh, soil incorporation involves four steps: applying wastes to soil, mixing for aeration, adding nutrients, and remixing periodically. The farmed area must be 1.5 meters above the water table and should be 150 meters from any potable water sources. The soil should be periodically monitored to a depth of 3 feet to check for migration of contaminants. The process can be accelerated by aerobic composting, but this process requires containment, protection from rain, and bulking agents to keep the material porous. W. Wesley Eckenfelder, Jr., in "Economic Alternatives for Industrial Waste Treatment," in *Environmental Quality and Society,* ed. Richard A. Tybout (Columbus: Ohio State, 1975), mentions two other methods of speeding up soil incorporation: using pure oxygen and multistaging the process to make use of the higher reaction rates in initial stages.

41. Eckenfelder, "Economic Alternatives for Industrial Waste Treatment."

42. Fowler, *Energy and the Environment.*

43. Steger and Bowermaster, *Saving the Earth.*

44. Eckenfelder, "Economic Alternatives for Industrial Waste Treatment."

45. Carl G. Schwarzer and David L. Storm, "Resource Recovery in California—An Alternative to Disposal of Hazardous Wastes," *Toxic Substances Journal* 2 (Summer 1980).

46. Maugh, "Hazardous Wastes Technology Is Available."

47. Ibid.

Chapter 4

1. A few remarks about the limits of this principle are in order. It is not meant to resolve all moral dilemmas, for several reasons. First, what must be assessed are the on-

balance, long-term likely effects of courses of action, rather than the effects of individual actions. In some sense a dentist leaves the world worse by drilling a hole in her patient's tooth, though the patient will be better off, ultimately, as a result of the whole course of treatment. Since some ambiguity always exists about what counts as a "course of action," we cannot apply the principle too rigidly.

Second, not leaving the world worse than one found it is neither a sufficient nor a necessary condition for right action. We might find ourselves in a "no-win" situation, in which any decision we might make will leave the world somewhat worse than we found it. Moreover, in some cases other moral considerations are more pressing. For example, a course of action that would make the world slightly worse might be required to avoid violating someone's rights. Rule-utilitarian considerations might force us to choose a course the result of which will leave the world worse than we found it. And of course some small "worsenings" are permissible in the course of a life generally devoted to improving the world. To take the extreme case, a saint is entitled to some small pleasures that have tiny detrimental effects on the world.

Third, there will be real disagreement about what counts as being "worse." In part this is because agents must make difficult on-balance, long-term assessments of the probable effects of their actions and in part because people disagree about the values in terms of which such assessments are made. In some cases, it is reasonably clear that a given course of action would make the world worse. In others, substantial disagreement will occur, and each individual has no choice but to act according to her own best judgment, informed by relevant facts and arguments. Some possible actions fall into the "gray area" about which we have no reasonable grounds for strong conviction. Whether acting within this gray area is permissible depends on what is at stake—how bad is the risk, and how great the potential benefit?

My point is that the duty to try to ensure that one's participation in the world does not leave it a worse place is something individuals must consider and address. The Ford executive must ask himself, ''Is the way of life made possible by the automobile worth 50,000 deaths a year?'' This question is difficult and perhaps unanswerable, but it cannot, in good faith, be avoided.

2. Many writers on business ethics distinguish between ''shareholders'' of a corporation and ''stakeholders'' in a corporation. The stakeholders are those who are significantly affected by the corporation's activities. Stakeholders include employees, clients, customers, consumers, store owners whose business depends upon employee's paychecks, and residents whose air and water might be contaminated by the corporation. It is often argued that corporations have duties to stakeholders as well as shareholders. While this may be true, it creates a dichotomy between providers (shareholders) and dependents (stakeholders), and it is tempting to think that the claim providers have on the corporation is stronger than the claim dependents have. I think a stronger argument can be made that corporations have duties to the community by distinguishing between the specific capital that stockholders provide and the opportunity capital the community provides. If we look at it this way, the relationship that shareholders have to the corporation is the same in kind as the relationship the community has to the corporation; both are providers without which the corporation could not operate.

3. Information for this example is based on W. Michael Hoffman, ''The Ford Pinto,'' in *Business Ethics: Readings and Cases in Corporate Morality,* ed. W. Michael Hoffman and Jennifer Mills Moore (New York: McGraw-Hill, 1984).

4. Mark Dowie, "Pinto Madness," *Mother Jones,* September-October 1977.

5. At the very least, it might be argued, Ford should have revealed to consumers that tests demonstrate that the standard Pinto tank ruptures at rear-end collisions of 20 mph and should have given consumers the option of purchasing the extra part. Richard T. de George points out in "Ethical Responsibilities of Engineers in Large Organizations, *Business and Professional Ethics Journal* 1 (Fall 1981), reprinted in *Ethics and the Professions,* ed. David Appelbaum and Sarah Verone Lawton (Englewood Cliffs, N.J.: Prentice-Hall, 1990), on p. 284, "If I choose to take a risk to save $6.65, it is my risk and my $6.65. But if Ford saves the $6.65 and I take the risk, then I clearly lose." Here it cannot reasonably be argued that consumers "vote with their dollars," since they were unaware of their options. In general, says de George on page 287, "the assumption that American drivers are more interested in styling than safety is a decision that has been made for them, not by them."

6. Cf. John P. Kavanagh, "Ethical Issues in Plant Relocation," in *Ethical Theory and Business,* ed. Tom Beauchamp and Norman Bowie, 3d ed. (Englewood Cliffs, N.J.: Prentice-Hall, 1988), pp. 106– 12.

7. Obviously, the situation becomes less clear if the Smallville plant is not profitable, or if Delta's decision is to open a new plant that would revitalize Littleville, which is currently depressed, or if the extra productivity resulting from closing the Smallville plant is large, since these factors make it less clear that closing the Delta plant creates more overall hardship.

8. For example, when Stroh's Brewery acquired Schlitz in 1982, Stroh's, a major Detroit employer for seventy years, decided to close its own Detroit breweries, which were inefficient compared to the newly acquired Schlitz breweries.

Detroit's unemployment rate stood at 9 percent. Stroh's spent $1.5 million, supplemented by $600,000 of government funds, in a program to find new jobs for the displaced employees. The program involved lobbying of employers by Peter Stroh, as well as "orientation, counseling, job skills workshops, skills testing, and training in resume preparation and interviewing." Virtually all of the Stroh's employees found new jobs (at a cost of $2,000 per worker). Other ameliorative strategies include finding a purchaser for the old facilities and adaptive reuse of the old facilities. (Desjardins and McCall, eds., *Contemporary Issues in Business Ethics,* p. 477.)

9. William Blackstone, *Philosophy and Environmental Ecology* (Athens: University of Georgia Press, 1972), excerpted in *Ethical Issues in Business,* ed. Thomas Donaldson and Patricia Werhane, 2d ed. (Englewood Cliffs, N.J.: Prentice-Hall, 1983), p. 369.

10. P. V. Pumphrey, "Chase Manhattan Bank, N.A.: A Case Narrative in Company Values," in *Business Ethics,* ed. Hoffman and Moore, p. 208.

11. Jones may be tempted to deny that her ad campaign would make the world worse. One can always find *some* benefit to any course of action, and it is tempting to say "But think of the extra jobs the stimulus to the economy may produce" or "Perhaps those who smoke high-tar cigarettes will smoke fewer of them." But such remarks ring hollow. Unless Jones is a fool, she cannot honestly believe that her campaign will not result in more cases of emphysema and lung cancer or that a few possible extra jobs balance out the resulting terrible suffering and numerous deaths. No one who looks at the situation clearly and honestly can deny that, overall, in authorizing the product and ad campaign, Jones will make the world a place of greater suffering. The fact remains that no one currently desires to smoke cigarettes that

contain higher levels of tar and nicotine, and no one will smoke them unless Jones sets out to induce them to do so by playing on their fears. If her ad campaign succeeds, many people will not live as long as they otherwise would, and the additional cases of emphysema and lung cancer caused by smoking He-Man cigarettes will lead to great suffering that would otherwise have been avoided. Thus, Jones must admit that she is quite deliberately setting out to bring about a worse world.

12. See, for example, Milton Friedman, ''The Social Responsibility of Business Is to Increase Its Profits,'' *New York Times Magazine,* September 13, 1970, reprinted in Raziel Abelson and Marie-Louise Friquegnon, *Ethics for Modern Life,* 3d ed. (New York: St. Martin's Press, 1987), pp. 281–87. See also the lengthy discussion of this issue in Alan H. Goldman, *The Moral Foundations of Professional Ethics* (Totowa, N.J.: Rowman and Littlefield, 1980). Since Friedman's article is often reprinted, it is worth pointing out a few flaws in his argument. Friedman argues that executives are agents of the stockholders hired for the express purpose of making a profit. Thus, says Friedman, an executive who uses stockholders' money to support the arts is imposing a tax on the stockholders. Similarly, an executive who spends stockholders' money on, for example, a nonmandated stack scrubber is imposing environmental restrictions on the stockholders. Friedman argues that only the legislature has the right to impose a tax or to impose environmental restrictions. Thus, it is improper for an executive to spend corporate money supporting the arts or instituting nonmandatory environmental safeguards unless those actions ultimately will maximize profits. In short, executives have a duty to maximize profits by any legal means. (While Friedman does suggest that executives keep within customary norms, this restriction tends to disappear from his discussions of actual cases.)

This argument is based on the importance of freedom. But unless corporations can be trusted to be good citizens, society must restrict and regulate every aspect of corporate behavior. For example, it seems to follow from Friedman's position that if a company can save a small amount of money by dumping poison in a reservoir, it ought to do so, provided the dumping is not illegal, runs no risk of litigation, and will not hurt sales. If executives really thought as Friedman suggests they should, the only way society could prevent its members from being poisoned in this way would be to generate a long list of restrictions, perform constant inspections to make sure that no new safety hazards are emerging, and so forth. In short, rather than being a recipe for greater freedom, Friedman's position is a recipe for more governmental interference than any socialist would wish for.

Expressed another way, the precondition for freedom is responsibility. If executives cannot be trusted to use common sense in being good citizens, citizens cannot afford to allow them much free rein. Thus, Friedman's position is self-defeating: his recommendation, meant to respect freedom, would actually decrease freedom. In any case, my argument that society provides the opportunity capital without which corporations could not function shows that executives' duty to make profits for stockholders is counterbalanced by their duty to society to be good citizens.

13. Frank Collins, "The Special Responsibility of Engineers," *Annals of the New York Academy of Sciences* 196 (1973), Article 10, pp. 448–50, reprinted in *Engineering Professionalism and Ethics,* ed. Schaub and Pavlovic (New York: John Wiley and Sons, 1983), p. 83.

14. See also Graham Haydon, "On Being Responsible," *Philosophical Quarterly* 28 (1978): 46–57.

15. Martin and Schinzinger, *Ethics in Engineering,* p. 63.

16. Ibid., p. 67.

17. In fact, Martin and Schinzinger themselves point out on pages 68–69 four features of modern engineering that help create a split between what one does and moral accountability for what one does: (1) the fragmentation of work means that the final product is removed, physically and psychologically, from what the individual engineer does, (2) diffusion of accountability, (3) "pressure to move on to a new project before the current one has been operating long enough to be observed carefully," and (4) a profusion of malpractice suits creates "a crippling preoccupation with legalities . . . [that] makes one wary of becoming morally involved in matters beyond one's strictly defined institutional role."

18. David Frew, "Pollution: Can People Be Innocent while Their Systems Are Guilty?" *Academy of Management Review* (March 1973), reprinted in *Ethics and the Professions,* ed. Appelbaum and Lawton, pp. 229–32. On page 230 Frew defines "synergism" as "that property by which . . . a system . . . takes on an identity [that] is essentially different from the aggregate of the parts of the system."

19. Frew, "Pollution," 231.

20. Interestingly, however, an National Science Foundation study of the 1960 Census showed that "73,000 technically qualified persons . . . had been missed because they had identified themselves with nontechnical positions, presumably managerial." Cited by Edwin Layton in "The Engineer and Business," in *Ethical Issues in the Professions,* ed. Peter Windt et al. (Englewood Cliffs, N.J.: Prentice-Hall, 1989), p. 487.

21. Cf. Albert Flores, "The Philosophical Basis of Engineering Codes of Ethics," in *Engineering and Humanities,* ed. James Schaub and Sheila Dickison (New York: John Wiley and Sons, 1982), p. 273: Flores states, "By accepting membership into a profession or any other institution, one

voluntarily takes on a set of role-defined duties above and beyond one's general moral obligations."

22. Cf. Abraham Flexner, "Is Social Work a Profession?" *School and Society* 1 (June 1915): 904, summarized by Morris Cogan in "The Problem of Defining a Profession," in *Engineering Professionalism and Ethics,* ed. Schaub and Pavlovic, p. 319: Flexner states that professions are characterized by "1) intellectual operations coupled with large individual responsibilities 2) raw materials drawn from science and learning 3) practical application 4) an educationally communicable technique 5) tendency toward self-organization, and 6) increasingly altruistic motivation."

Also cf. Martin Goland, "Can Professionalism Be Attained within the Corporate Structure?" in *Engineering Professionalism and Ethics,* ed. Schaub and Pavlovic, p. 286: He argues, "The virtues of professionalism are in independent thought, the creative dedication to the dual and compatible goals of advancing the employer's interests while serving the just needs of the society."

Also cf. the American Society of Chemical Engineers' amplification of its definition of a "profession," cited by Carl Nelson and Susan Peterson, "Ethical Decisions for Engineers: Systematic Avoidance of the Need for Confrontation," in *Engineering Professionalism and Ethics,* ed. Schaub and Pavlovic, p. 331: "A profession is a calling in which special knowledge and skill are used in a distinctly intellectual plane in the service of mankind, and in which the successful expression of creative ability and application of professional knowledge are the primary rewards. There is implied the application of the highest standards of excellence in the educational fields prerequisite to the calling, in the performance of services, and in the ethical conduct of its members."

Also cf. Lisa H. Newton, "Lawgiving for Professional Life: Reflections on the Place of the Professional Code," *Business and Professional Ethics Journal* (1981): 41–53, reprinted in *Professional Ideals,* ed. Albert Flores (Belmont, Calif.: Wadsworth, 1988), p. 48: She considers that professionals "possess a specialized art, skill or capacity, requiring long and difficult education and extended practice; they are employed full-time in the practice of that art . . . they render a service to individual clients and to society in the practice of the art."

Also cf. Lisa Newton, "Professionalization: The Intractable Plurality of Values," in *Profits and Professions,* ed. Wade L. Robinson, Michael S. Pritchard, and Joseph Ellin (Clifton, N.J.: Humana, 1983), reprinted in *Ethical Issues in the Professions,* ed. Windt et al., pp. 50–51: She asserts that two features of professionalism are "maximal competence in a certain area of knowledge or skill, and a moral commitment to the public good in that area." (This often results in "social award of a legitimate monopoly of practice.") A third "prominent feature" is "commitment on the part of individual professionals to the welfare and interests of individuals in their charge."

Also cf. William Sullivan, "Calling or Career: The Tension of Modern Professional Life," in *Professional Ideals,* ed. Flores, p. 41: He states that the original meaning of a "profession" is a calling, "a promise to enter on a distinct way of life, . . . a free act in response to a belief that one had received a 'call,' . . . and it meant a commitment to embody virtues central to the community's highest purposes."

Also cf. Edwin T. Layton, *The Revolt of the Engineers,* 2d ed. (Baltimore, Md.: Johns Hopkins University Press, 1986), pp. 1–9, reprinted as Layton, "The Engineer and Business," in *Ethical Issues in the Professions,* ed. Windt et al., pp. 483–84: He defines the values of professionalism as "autonomy, collegial control of professional work, and social responsibility,'' where the last means ''special responsibility to see that [one's] knowledge is used for the benefit of the community,'' that is, the use of ''esoteric knowledge . . . guided by a sense of public duty.''

23. Michael Bayles, *Professional Ethics* (Belmont, Calif.: Wadsworth, 1981), pp. 7–8.

24. For example, suppose all the owners of rental properties within a hundred miles of Midville offer tenants the same ''boilerplate'' five-year lease, according to which the landlord may raise the rent at will, and the tenant, who may not inspect the premises before signing the lease, must pay for any repairs or improvements upon which the landlord decides. Although this is a grossly unfair contract, Midville renters have no real choice but to sign it. Such a contract is called a ''contract of adhesion'' and is not enforceable.

25. Cf. Lisa Newton, ''Professionalization: The Intractable Plurality of Values,'' in which she describes on page 55 ''two candidates for the essence of 'professionalism,' two possible *raisons d'etre* for a profession: it can exist for the sake of excellence in the practice, or it can exist for the sake of profit for the practitioners. A third possible motivating principle . . . might be the direct service rendered to identifiable others.''

26. Martin and Schinzinger, *Ethics in Engineering,* 242. See also Edward Layton, *The Revolt of the Engineers* (Cleveland, Ohio: Case Western Reserve, 1971).

27. Some philosophers have argued that promoting good consequences is all that matters in ethics. Act utilitarians suggest that one should always perform the action that has the best overall consequences for everyone concerned. Rule utilitarians suggest that one should always follow the set of rules that would produce the best overall consequences if those rules were generally followed. Unlike act and rule

utilitarians, I treat the promotion of good consequences as one moral factor that must be weighed against others.

28. This corresponds to the difference between act and rule utilitarianism. Act utilitarians believe in doing the particular action, out of all those one could perform, that would produce the most utility (the best overall balance of happiness over unhappiness for everyone affected by one's action). Rule utilitarians advocate following the set of rules that would produce the most utility (balance of happiness over unhappiness for everyone) if those rules were generally followed.

29. The principle of universality is closely associated with the work of Immanuel Kant. Whereas Kant treated the principle as a test that every action must pass to be considered ethical, I treat the principle as one source of ethical decision making that must be weighed against others.

30. Other versions of the Golden Rule have parallel problems. For example, one version is "Don't do unto others what you would not have done to you." Now consider a physician who would not want to be told of a terminal illness. Since he would not want to be told, the Golden Rule seems to insist that he not inform a patient who does want to be told the truth about her condition. And this seems clearly wrong. Interestingly, another way of describing this example seems to get the Golden Rule off the hook. Perhaps what you really want is to have your wishes respected, so you should respect the wishes of the patient. Thus, the Golden Rule directs you to tell the patient who desires to be told. This shows that the Golden Rule is vague: how you describe the situation makes all the difference. Anyway, this strategy does not help with the second kind of problem: you do not want to be locked away (incapacitated), and you would not want to be incapacitated even if you had committed several muggings. Yet it is not wrong to protect innocent persons by incapacitating a

mugger just because you would not want to be incapacitated if you were a mugger.

The basic problems with the Golden Rule can be summarized simply. First, it is not always right to give people what they want (or what you would want if you were in their place). Second, people often want conflicting things, but the Golden Rule is supposed to apply to everyone. For example, if you have to decide between keeping a more senior employee or a more efficient employee, the Golden Rule does not help you. You would want the decision to be made on seniority were you in the shoes of the more senior employee, and you would want the decision to be made on merit were you in the shoes of the more efficient employee. Finally, there is always some way of describing an action so that you would want it done to you and some way of describing the same action so that you would not want it done to you.

31. To see this, ask yourself if anyone would really give up a full and prosperous life in which others are more prosperous for a miserable life in which everyone else is more miserable. No one would. What this shows is that what really matters is how good *your* life is, not whether others get ahead of you.

The same goes for revenge—people who make great personal sacrifices or take large personal risks to get revenge are not thinking clearly about what is important in life. No one really thinks that having a full and rich life is less important than making sure no one gets away with wronging or harming her.

Similarly, some people are dedicated to having videocassette recorders, large wardrobes, and a status car, to going to the ''right'' college, to outplaying their friends at golf, or to giving a ''better'' party than their neighbors. These people have not thought clearly and rationally about what matters in life. (See ''The Consumer Life versus the Life of Values'' in Chapter 1.)

32. Cf. Sullivan, "Calling or Career," p. 41: Sullivan defines "a practice" as "an activity socially organized and defined by impersonal standards through which certain goods are realized."

33. Similarly, if you do not "do-si-do" when you are supposed to, you are not square dancing. You may be having fun on the dance floor, and what you are doing when whirling your partner and displaying your fancy footwork may be more elegant and enjoyable than square dancing. But, to paraphrase Will Rogers, it ain't square dancing. If you want to square dance, you have to follow the rules. If you do not follow the rules, you are just not square dancing. If an accountant does not follow the rules governing company audits, she is not doing an audit. The information she comes up with may be interesting and useful. But it is not an audit. And a reporter who does not follow the "rules" of news reporting, who writes a biased story in highly charged language, may be writing an important and valuable "opinion piece." What he is not doing is covering the news.

34. This version of rule utilitarianism is suggested by Rawls' famous paper, "Two Concepts of Rules," by Mabbott's theory of punishment, and explicitly defended by Stephen Toulmin in *The Role of Reason in Ethics.*

Chapter 5

1. Martin and Schinzinger, in *Ethics in Engineering,* give this definition of whistleblowing on page 200: "1. Information is conveyed outside approved organizational channels. . . . 2. The information being revealed is new[.] . . . 3. [The information] concerns what the whistleblower believes is a significant moral problem[, and] 4. [The information] . . . is conveyed intentionally with the aim of drawing attention to the problem."

2. Ronald Duska, "Whistleblowing II," in *Ethical Issues in the Professions,* ed. Windt et al., p. 321.

3. Richard T. de George, *Business Ethics* (New York: MacMillan, 1982), p. 162. See also Ralph Nader, "An Anatomy of Whistle Blowing," in *Whistle Blowing,* ed. Ralph Nader et al. (1972) for a list of eight questions the whistleblower must ask.

4. Westrum, *Technologies and Society,* p. 315.

5. Samuel C. Florman, "Beyond Whistleblowing," *Technology Review* (July 1989): 19.

6. Not everyone would agree with me, of course. Milton Friedman's view, discussed in "The Duty to Leave the World No Worse" in Chapter 4, suggests that the job of executives and their agents is to make a profit for their shareholders. It is up to the government to attend to the public welfare, not the engineers and executives, since the extra costs required to prevent pollution are tantamount to a tax on the shareholders of Y company, and only a democratically elected government may impose a tax. Thus, engineers and executives should do everything legally permissible to increase profits. It seems to follow from Friedman's view that it is up to the Department of Environmental Quality to pick a suitable sampling site, and if the department chooses poorly, it is not the company's problem. As I pointed out earlier, however, Friedman's view has many difficulties.

7. Westrum, *Technologies and Society,* pp. 313–14.

8. Ibid., pp. 253–55.

9. Roger Boisjoly, "Ethical Decisions—Morton Thiokol and the Space Shuttle *Challenger,*" ASME Paper 87-WA/TS-4 (New York: American Society of Mechanical Engineers, December 1987), p. 11.

10. Source: Stephen H. Unger, *Controlling Technology: Ethics and the Responsible Engineer* (New York: Holt, Rinehart and Winston, 1982).

11. Westrum, *Technologies and Society,* p. 314.

12. Source: Unger, *Controlling Technology.*

13. Ibid.

14. Ibid., p. 61.

15. *Louisiana Engineer,* December 1989, p. 11.

16. Philip Alger, N. A. Christensen, and Sterling P. Olmsted, *Ethical Problems in Engineering* (New York: John Wiley and Sons, 1965), p. 126.

Chapter 6

1. Cf. "Conflicts of Interest Pose No Big Problem," *Chemical and Engineering News,* October 1961: This article indicates that examples of conflict of interest situations include "owning a financial interest in or holding a position with" or "accepting fees, gifts, entertainment, loans or other favors from" a "supplier, agent, customer or competitor"; "acquiring an interest in a business, real estate, or other facilities in which the company may be interested"; and "speculating on the basis of inside information."

2. Robert E. Frederick, "Conflict of Interest," in *Business Ethics,* ed. Milton Snoeyenbos et al. (Prometheus, 1983), pp. 125–34.

3. Alger et al., *Ethical Problems in Engineering.*

4. Martin and Schinzinger, *Ethics in Engineering,* p. 177.

5. Michael S. Baram, "Trade Secrets: What Price Loyalty?" *Harvard Business Review* 46 (November-December 1968): 66–74, reprinted as "Protecting Trade Secrets" in *Ethical Issues in the Professions,* ed. Windt et al., p. 308.

6. A similar case can be found in Philip Kohn and Roy Hughson, "Perplexing Problems in Engineering Ethics," *Chemical Engineering* 87 (May 1980): 100–107.

7. William Shaw and Vincent Barry, *Moral Issues in Business,* 4th ed. (Belmont, Calif.: Wadsworth, 1989), pp.

305–6. See also Jeffrey A. Fadiman, "A Business Traveler's Guide to Gifts and Bribes," *Harvard Business Review* (1986), reprinted in Shaw and Barry, *Moral Issues in Business,* pp. 328–37.

8. Cited in *Business Ethics,* ed. Snoeyenbos et al.

9. Alger et al., *Ethical Problems in Engineering,* p. 136.

10. Ibid., p. 115.

11. Cf. ibid., p. 114: "Most reputable organizations allow their engineering employees to publish papers covering important new discoveries or advances in the art after patent protection has been received, if possible, and after reasonable time has been allowed for initial use of the new ideas by those responsible for them."

Chapter 7

1. Bruce F. Gordon and Ian C. Ross, "Professionals and the Corporation," *Research Management* 5, no. 6 (1962): 493–505, reprinted in *Engineering Professionalism and Ethics,* ed. Schaub and Pavlovic, pp. 149–57.

2. R. P. Cort, *Communicating with Employees* (Englewood Cliffs, N.J.: Prentice-Hall, 1963), p. 10, cited in James M. Humber, "Honesty in Organizational Communication," in *Business Ethics,* ed. Snoeyenbos et al., pp. 175–84.

3. Humber, "Honesty in Organizational Communication," pp. 175–84.

4. Tom Peters and Nancy Austin, *A Passion for Excellence* (Random House, 1985; reprinted by Warner 1986), p. 6.

5. Ibid., pp. 10, 12, 13, 18, 20.

6. Ibid., pp. 35, 27.

7. Ibid., p. 39.

8. Srully Blotnick, *The Corporate Steeple Chase* (Penguin, 1984).

9. Ibid., pp. 92, 90.

10. Ibid., p. 103.

11. D. Allan Firmage, "Management/Employee Ethics in Engineering Offices," *Professional Issues in Engineering* 115 (January 1989): 53–58.

12. Ibid., p. 57.

13. W. H. Roadstrum, *Excellence in Engineering* (New York: John Wiley and Sons, 1967), p. 181.

14. Ibid., p. 180.

15. David Ewing, "What Business Thinks about Employee Rights," *Harvard Business Review* 55 (1977): 234–35, quoted in Martin and Schinzinger, *Ethics in Engineering,* p. 212.

16. *NSPE Guidelines to Professional Employment for Engineers and Scientists,* 2d ed., republished in *Professional Engineer* 50 (June 1980): 15–21.

17. Milton Snoeyenbos and Robert Almeder, "Ethical Hiring Practices," in *Business Ethics,* ed. Snoeyenbos et al., p. 199.

18. Gary Dessler, *Personnel Management,* 2d ed. (Reston, 1981), pp. 136–42, cited in *Business Ethics,* ed. Snoeyenbos et al., pp. 205–6.

19. Alger et al., *Ethical Problems in Engineering,* p. 109.

Chapter 8

1. For example, Louisiana Administrative Code 46-LXI, Chapter 21, Section 2105.C, states that "registrants shall undertake to perform professional engineering or land surveying services only after having been selected on the basis of competency and qualifications. Registrants shall not solicit or submit fee proposals prior to selection."

List of Cases

case 1:	The overheard remark	10
case 2:	Carcinogenic lipstick	53
case 3:	The AIDS drug	55
case 4:	The Conrail train	55
case 5:	The Dalkon Shield	56
case 6:	Narbitol	57
case 7:	Sandbagging a rival	63
case 8:	Environmentally harmful products	78
case 9:	Environmentally harmful manufacturing	80
case 10:	Environmental accidents	81
case 11:	Waste materials	81
case 12:	Using non-renewable resources	83
case 13:	The cooling system	83
case 14:	The tardy employee	91
case 15:	Informing employees of outside opportunities	93
case 16:	Promoting ''my kind of person''	94
case 17:	Ford Pinto	98
case 18:	Relocating a plant	99
case 19:	He-Man Cigarettes	102
case 20:	Freedom of speech	108
case 21:	Giving credit when due	133
case 22:	When to bid (I)	143
case 23:	''Adjusting'' the records	144
case 24:	Keeping a promise	145
case 25:	Cadmium and outflow sampling	157
case 26:	Going easy on safety assessments	159
case 27:	The B.A.R.T. case	159

case 28:   The Challenger disaster   160
case 29:   The DC-10   161
case 30:   Cost overruns (C-5A Galaxy)   162
case 30:   The Surry nuclear power facility   163
case 32:   Competence   164
case 33:   Sales honesty   174
case 34:   Trade secrets   180
case 35:   When to bid (II)   184
case 36:   The expense-paid trip   184
case 37:   The personal discount   184
case 38:   Discussing one vendor with another   186
case 39:   Using an unsuccesful bidder's idea   186
case 40:   Owning stock   187
case 41:   Personal use of company facilities   188
case 42:   ''Rescuing'' from the garbage dump   189
case 43:   Copying software   190
case 44:   Taking home a pencil   190
case 45:   Publicizing your work   190
case 46:   Moonlighting   215
case 47:   Dismissal for non-work-related conduct   216
case 48:   Giving reasons for dismissal   218
case 49:   Hiring away   218
case 50:   Complaints about one's successor (I)   219
case 51:   Complaints about one's successor (II)   219

Index

Accountability, principles of, 77, 86, 112–14, 151, 193, 268

Acid rain, 66, 68

Alger, Philip, 178, 184, 276, 278

Almeder, Robert, 212

American Society of Chemical Engineers, 269

Amoco, 82

Apple, 198

Applegate, Daniel, 161–62

Aral Sea project, 65–66

Arguments from recognition, 253–54

Aristotle, 43, 44

Atlantic Richfield, 82

Austin, Nancy, 197–98

Autonomy, 20, 110–11, 112, 121, 169, 208, 213, 216

Baram, Michael, 180

Barry, Vincent, 183

Battle, when to fight, 18–19, 86–89, 99, 151, 155, 157

Bayles, Michael, 118

Bazelon, David, 256

Beauchamp, Tom, 264

Bidding, 141–42, 143–44, 183–91, 206, 225

Biological diversity, 67

Blackstone, William, 265

Blotnick, Srully, 198–201

Boisjoly, Roger, 160–61

Bonuses, problems with, 196

Bottom-line thinking, problems with, 7–8, 196

Bowermaster, John, 260, 261

Bowie, Norman, 264

Buchholz, Rogene, 256

Bush, Vannevar, 253

Cadmium, 80, 157–58

Campbell's Soup, 198

CFCs, 65, 76

Cogan, Morris, 269

Collins, Frank, 112

Community atmosphere, 5, 6, 7, 8–9, 11–13, 60–63, 86, 91, 92, 93–94, 121, 123–24, 151–52, 188, 194, 195–99, 202–7, 208, 212–13, 214, 216–18, 219–20

Confidentiality, 140, 141, 151–52, 177–81, 190–91, 214, 231, 277

Conflict of interest, 144, 175–77, 183–90, 206, 215, 225

Consumer life, 13–18, 96, 103, 134, 273

Contracts of adhesion, 119, 271

Corporate climate, 6, 8

Cort, R. P., 197

Deciding in the face of uncertainty, 53–54
De George, Richard, 150–51, 264
Desjardins, Joseph, 260, 265
Dessler, Gary, 213
Donaldson, Thomas, 265
Dow Chemical, 82
Dowie, Mark, 98
Duska, Ronald, 150

Eckenfelder, 261
Endangered Species Act, 71–72
Engineering, definition/nature of, 42, 44, 64, 252–53, 254–55
Environment. See Nature, partnership with
Equal Employment Opportunity Commission, 207–8
Evans, R. J., 251–52
Ewing, David, 278

Fadiman, Jeffrey, 277
Fairness, 20, 89–94, 124, 125, 136, 142–43, 151–52, 173, 182, 195, 203, 205, 208, 212–13, 218, 219–20, 226
Firmage, Allan, 201
Fitzgerald, A. Ernest, 162
Fleming, John, 6
Flexner, Abraham, 269
Flores, Albert, 268–69
Florman, Samuel, 157, 252, 256, 259
Fowler, John, 257, 261
Frederick, Robert, 177
Freeman, Myrick, 260
Frew, David, 113
Friedman, Milton, 266, 275

Gaia theory, 67–68
Geocentric views of nature, 258–59
Gobas, Harvey, 256
Goland, Martin, 269
Golden Rule, 89, 132–34, 186, 272–73
Goldman, Alan, 266
Gordon, Bruce, 192

Hall, Newman, 252
Hanke, Steve, 259
Hanson, Kirk, 251
Hargrove, Eugene, 258
Haveman, Robert, 260
Haydon, Graham, 254, 267
Hewlett-Packard, 63, 198
Highway construction, 71
Hiring: from another firm, 126, 214–15, 218; and promotion, 9–10, 154, 203, 208, 212–13
Hoffman, W. Michael, 263
Holbrook, George, 253
Honeywell, 184
Houston, Carl, 163
Hughson, Roy, 276
Human progress (welfare), 54, 58, 64, 77, 115, 117, 173, 180, 181–82, 190
Humber, James, 197
Hume, David, 253
Hynes, Patricia, 257, 260

Institute of Electrical and Electronics Engineers, 166

Jones, Donald, 6
Joseph, Lawrence, 257
Justice. See *Fairness*

Kant, Immanuel, 105, 272
Kavanaugh, John, 264
Killian, James R. Jr., 252
Kneese, Allen, 260
Kohn, Philip, 276
Kotlyankov, V. M., 257

Law, 7, 32, 50, 71, 107, 138, 153,
    168–71, 181–82, 188, 203, 206,
    207, 211, 212–13, 217, 221–22,
    225, 226–27, 228, 258, 268,
    278
Layton, Edward, 268, 270, 271
Leaving the world no worse, duty
    to, 54, 94–104, 121, 151–52,
    157, 261–63
Levi Strauss, 198
Locke, John, 42
Lovelock, James, 257

Mahoney, Richard, 72
Manheim, Marvin, 256
Manipulation, 90, 93, 105
Margulis, Lynn, 257
Martin, Mike, and Schinzinger,
    Roland, 48, 112–13, 120, 179,
    254, 255, 256, 268, 274, 278
Marx, Karl, 42
Maugh, Thomas H., II, 260, 261
McCall, John, 260, 265
Mercury, 80
Merrill, Sarah, 31
Milliken and Company, 198
Mobil, 82
Monsanto, 72

Nader, Ralph, 275
Natural, definition of, 69–70

Nature, partnership with (environ-
    ment), 43, 64–84, 100–101, 115,
    117, 158, 231
Nelson, Carl, 269
Newton, Lisa, 270, 271
NSPE, 278

Olmsted, Sterling P., 276
Opportunity capital (dual-investor
    model), 97, 263, 267
Ottoson, Gerals, 8
Ozone layer, 65, 67, 76

Passmore, John, 258
Pavlovic, K. R., 252
People's Express, 198
Peters, Tom, 197–98
Peterson, Susan, 269
Picture building, 253–54
Pilko, George, 73
Prisoner's dilemma, 62–63
Promoting good consequences.
    See *Utilitarianism*
Pumphrey, P. V., 101

Rawls, John, 274
Recycling, 76, 81–82, 260
Respect for persons, 89, 105–6,
    110
ReVelle, Penelope, and Charles,
    260
Rights of natural objects, 68,
    258
Roadstrum, W. H., 201–2
Ross, Ian, 192
Rubbermaid, 83
Rules, 4–6, 205, 215; when to
    break, 122–24, 135–46, 159,
    169, 178, 183

Safety, 27, 45–58, 78, 81, 87, 111,
    112, 115, 117, 130, 151, 154–
    55, 157–62, 163, 194, 224, 225,
    228, 231, 255–56
Sales ethics, 171–74, 222
Schwarzer, Carl, 261
Sea turtles, 71
Shaw, William, 183
Snoeyenbos, Milton, 212, 276
Societies, professional, 112, 120,
    164, 165–68, 190–91, 201
Stakeholders v. shareholders, 263
Steger, Will, 260, 261
Storm, David, 261
Stroh's Brewery, 264
Subordinates, dealing with, 89–94,
    101, 105, 106, 108–9, 122–24,
    133–34, 135, 145–46, 154, 176–
    77, 192–220
Sullivan, William, 270, 274

Tandem, 198
Technology: as practical wisdom,
    43–44, 253–54; not value neu-
    tral, 44
Thermosets, 76
Thompson, William, 257

3M, 198
Time Magazine, 102
Timsfors Pulp Mill, 82
Tirecycle, 81
Toulmin, Stephen, 274
Tredgold, Thomas, 254

Unger, Stephen, 165–67, 275, 276
Universality, principle of, 94, 125–
    30, 152–53, 169–70, 173, 191,
    272
Utilitarianism (promoting good
    consequences), 122–24, 131,
    137, 151, 163, 173, 182, 262,
    271–72, 274

Values, 14, 16–17, 23–24, 27, 41,
    134–35, 224, 231, 273

Waste disposal, 82–83, 261
Werhane, Patricia, 265
Westrum, Ron, 157, 256, 257
Whistleblowing, 87, 109, 149–63
Whitbeck, Caroline, 32
Wright, Frank Lloyd, 70

Young, John A., 257